BEETLEJUICE PUBLICATIONS
EST 2020
jORDAN MENDEZ

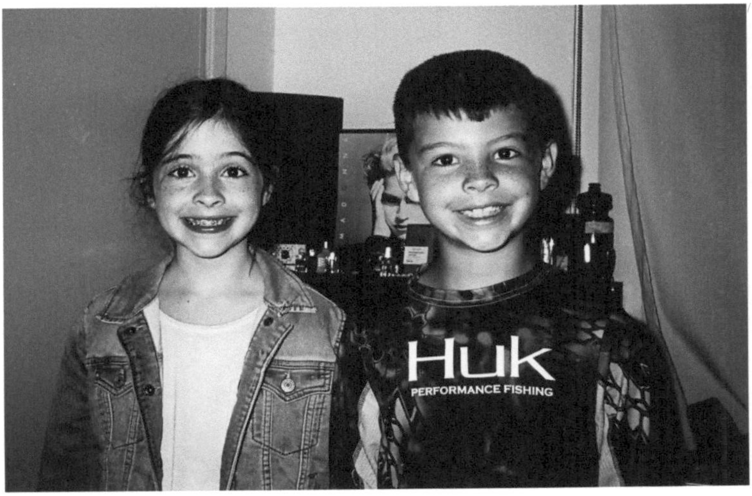

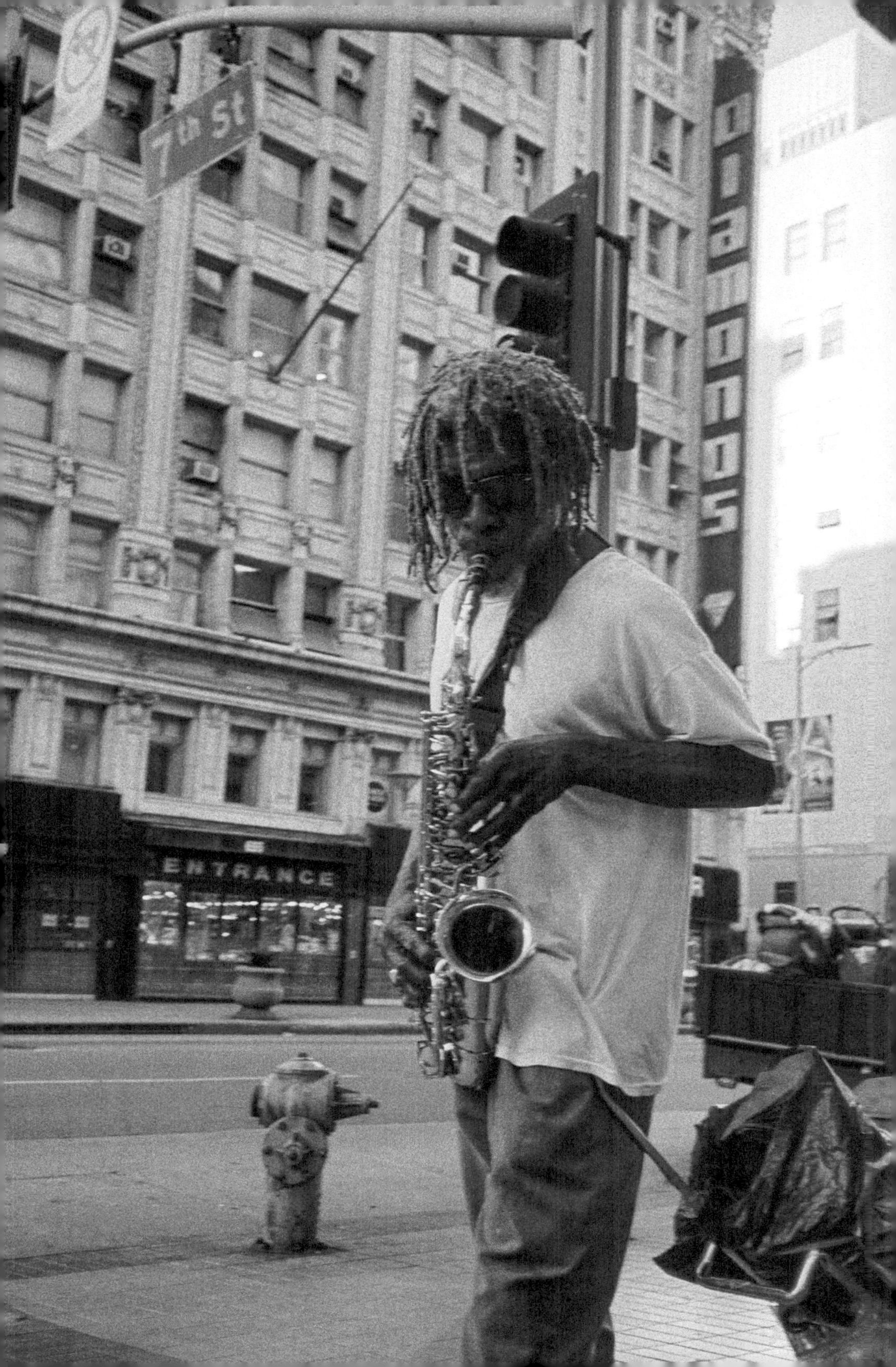
7th St
ENTRANCE

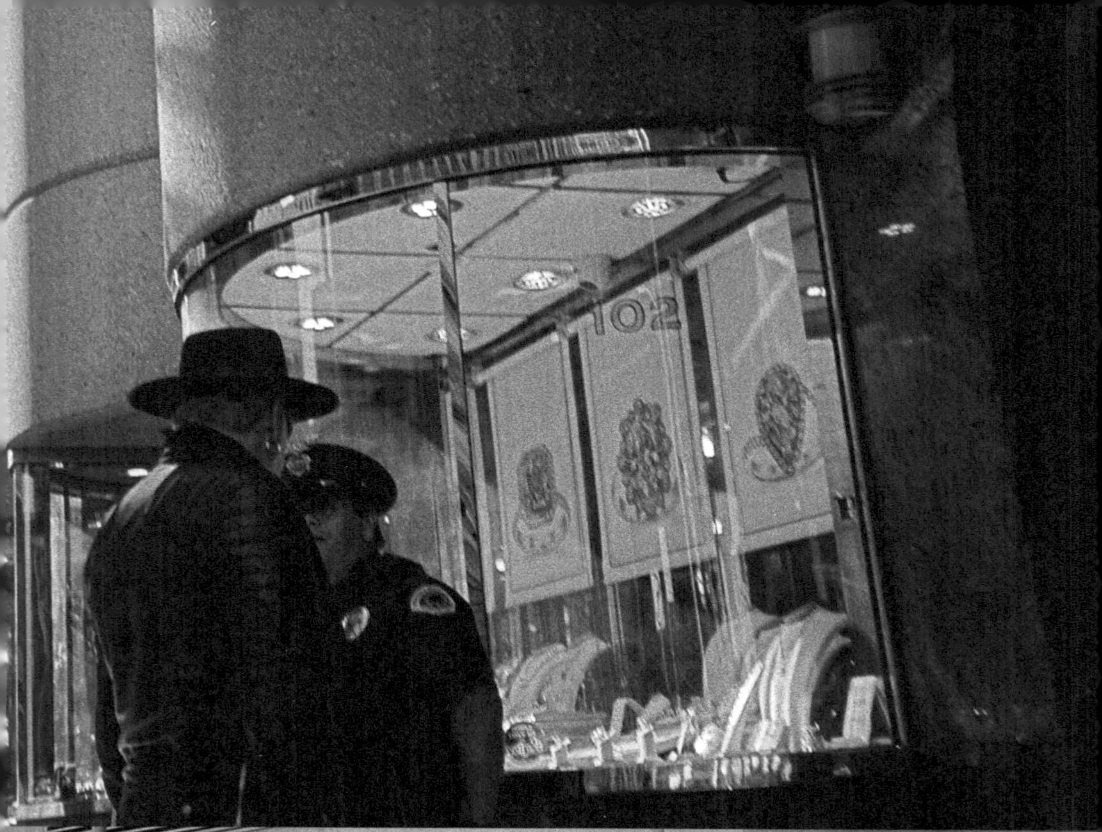
102

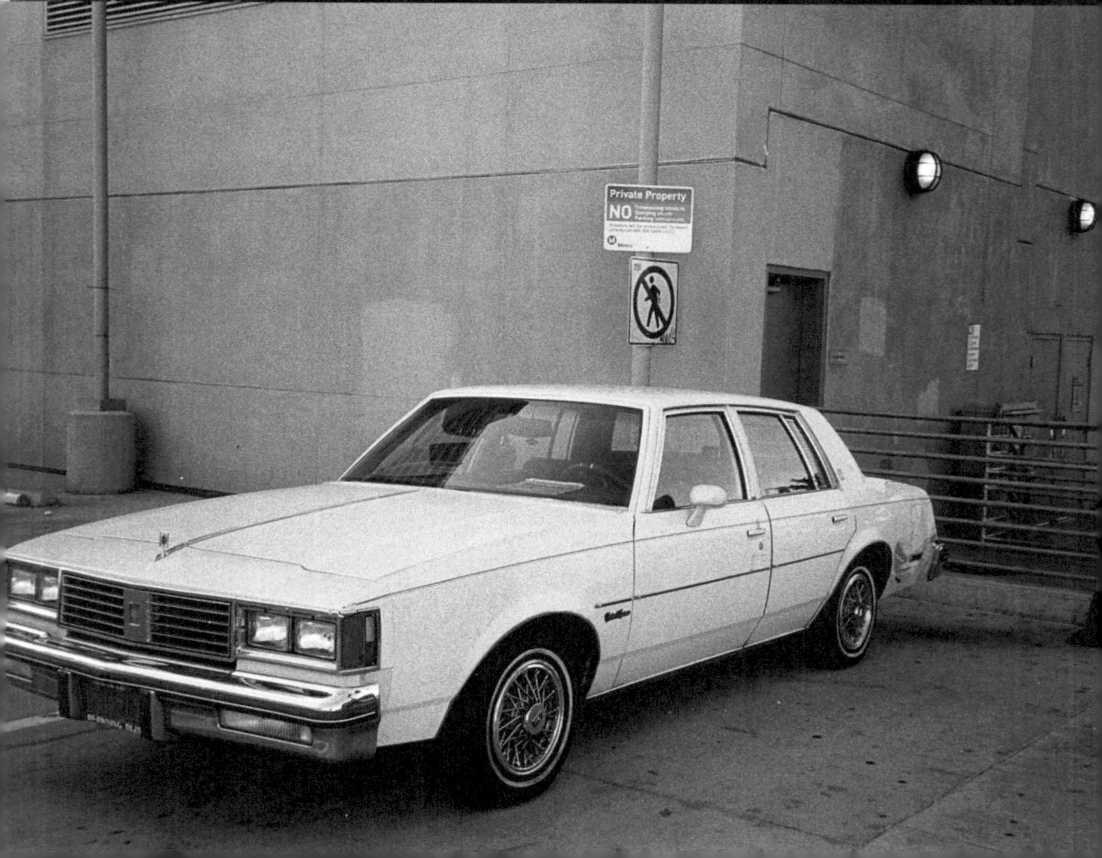
Private Property
NO

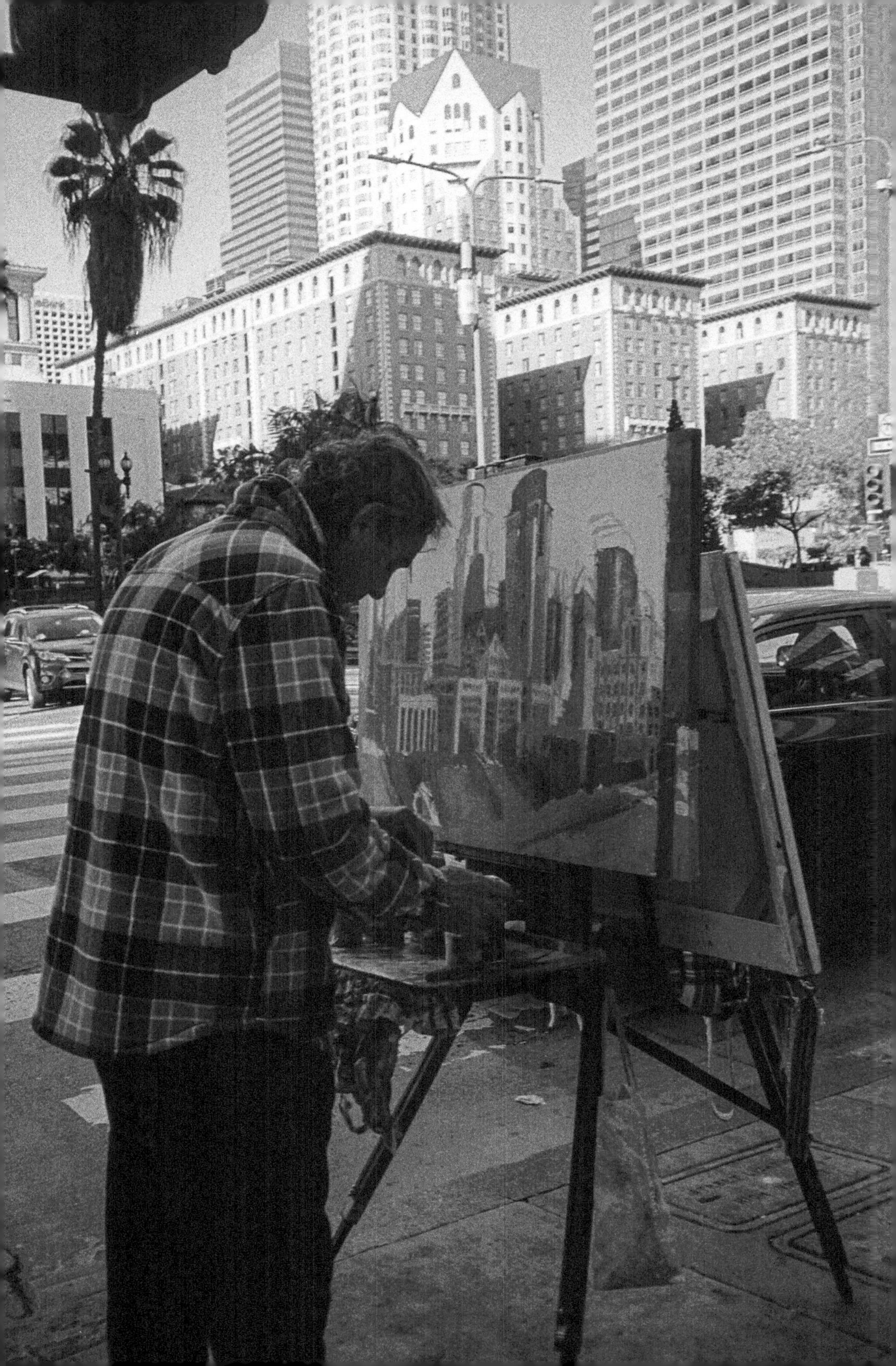

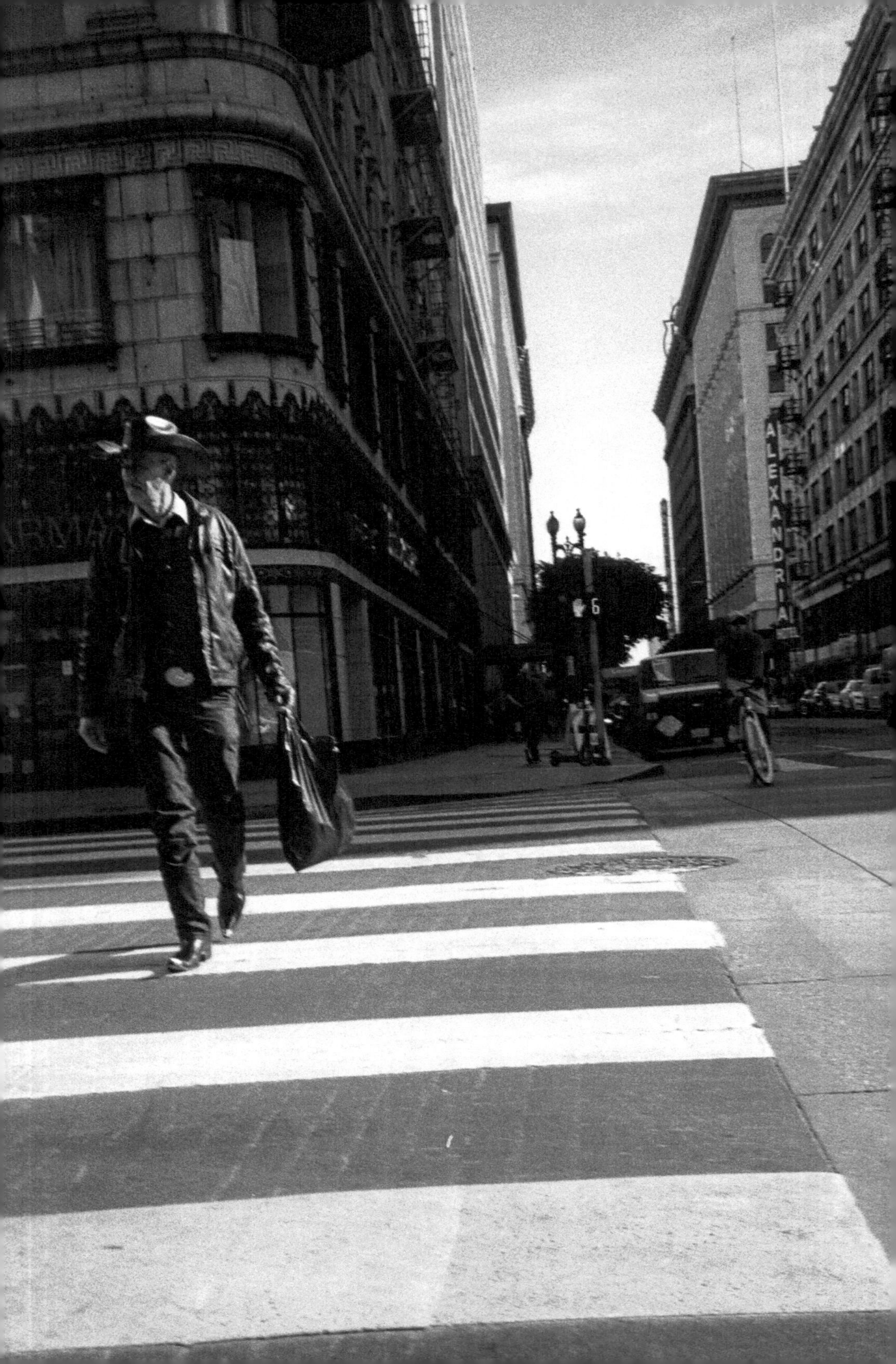
ALEXANDRIA
6

MAKE LESS MORE
MAKE LESS MORE
SNIPER

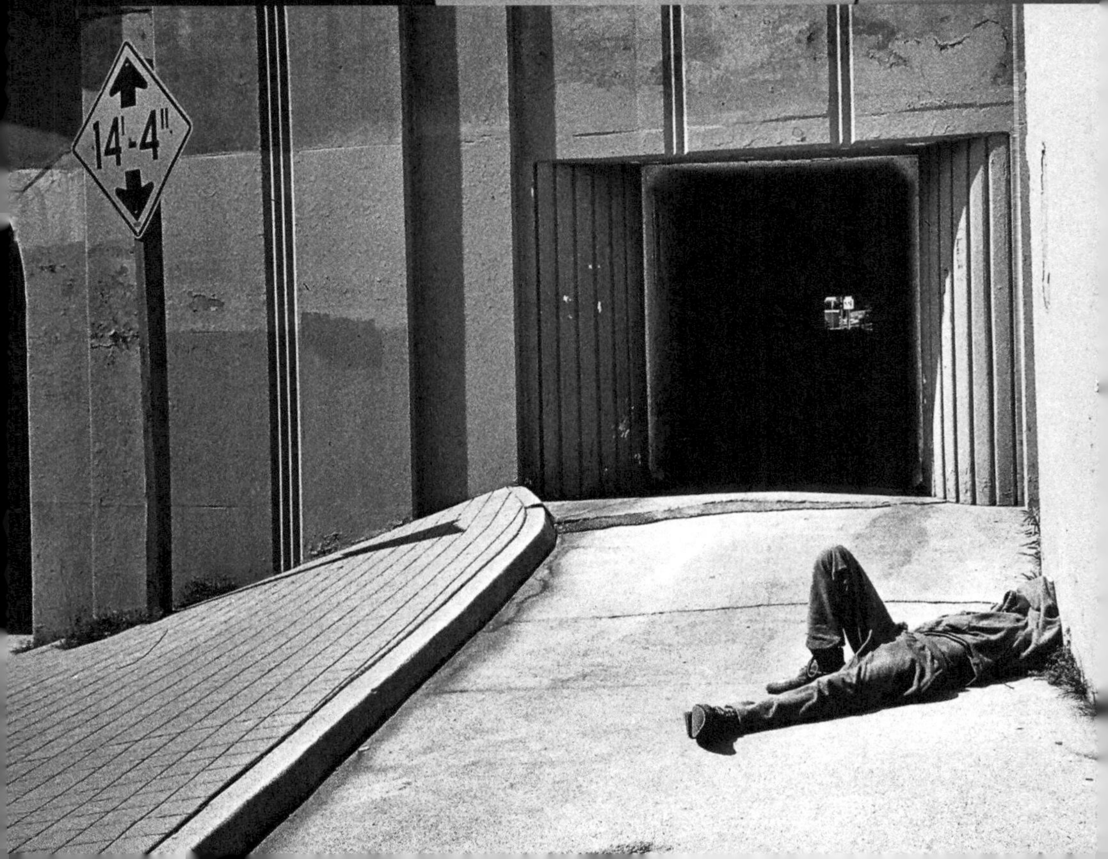
14'-4"

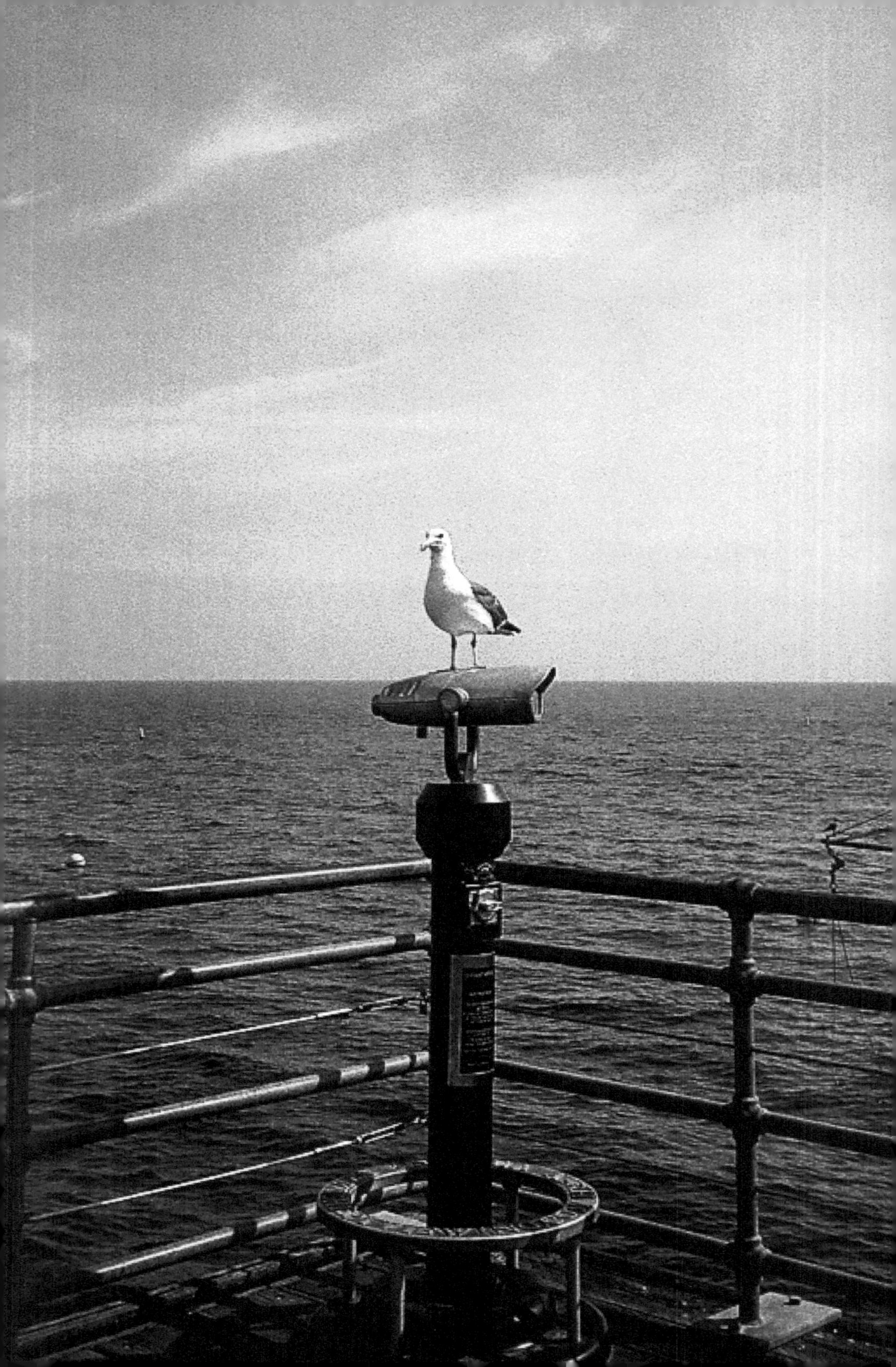

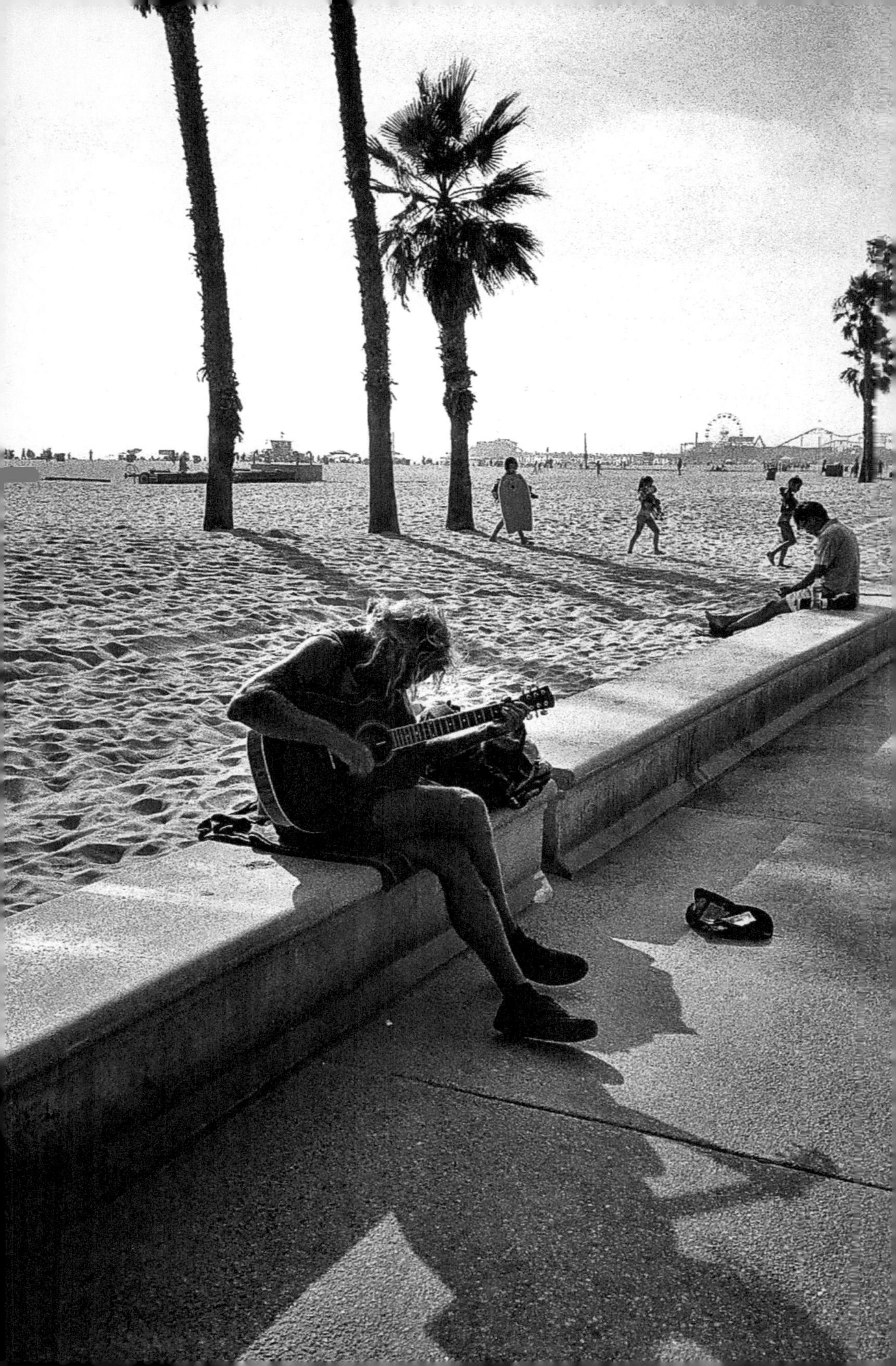

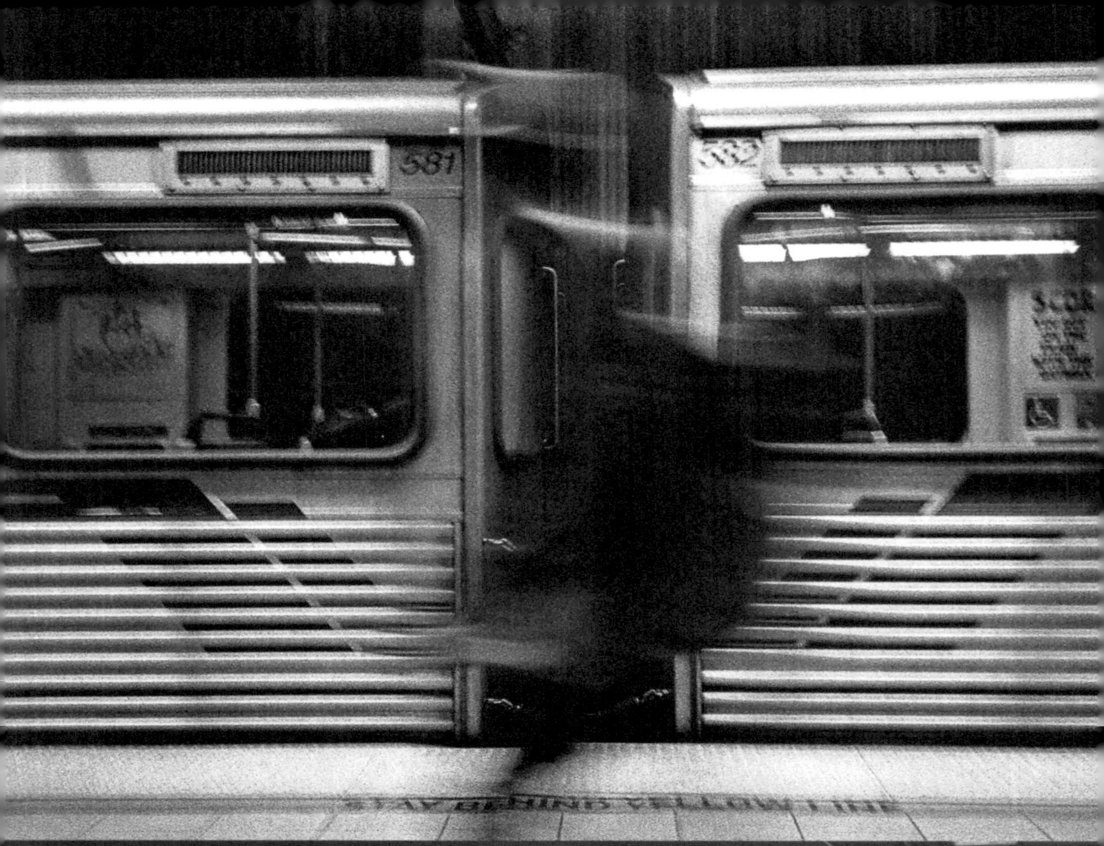
581

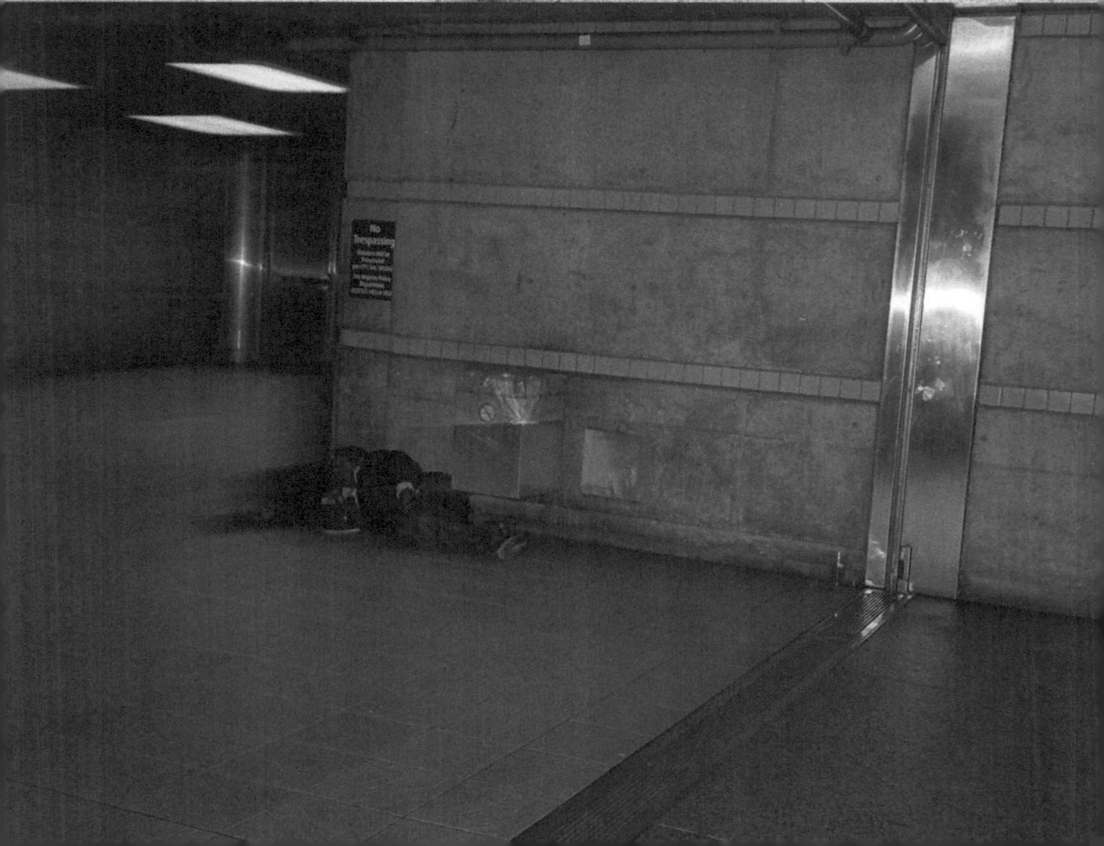
No Trespassing

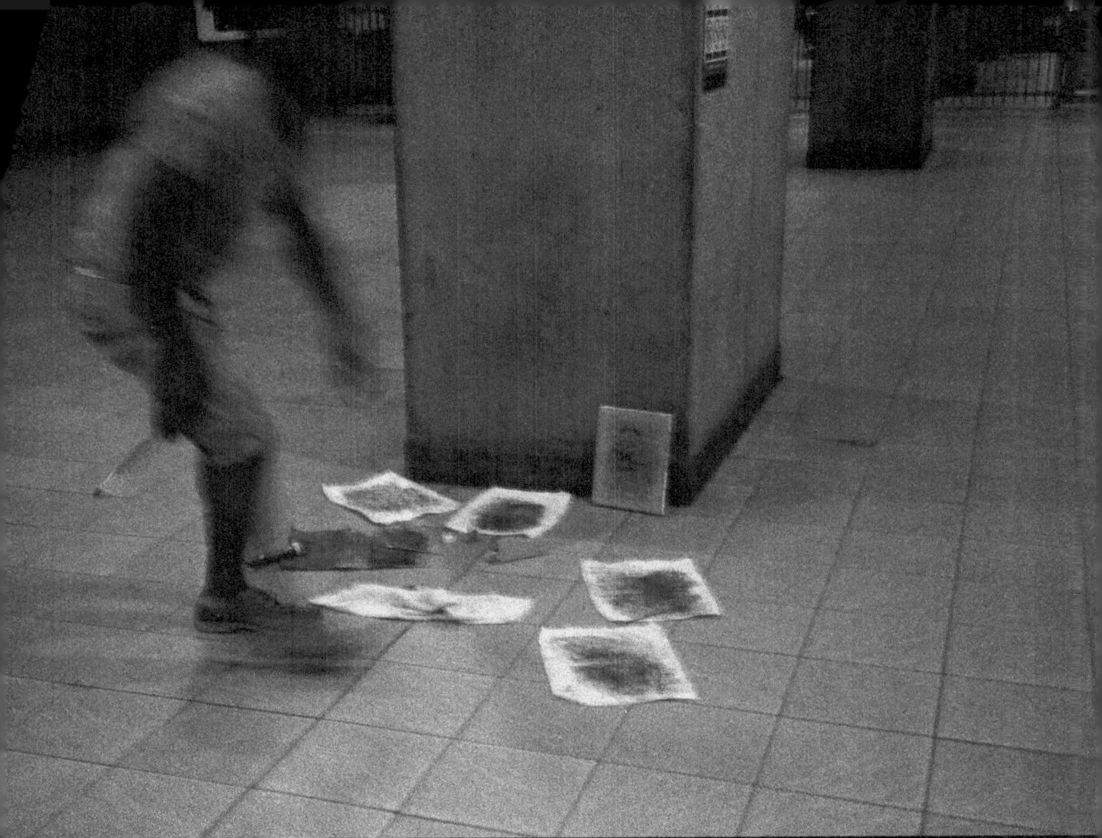

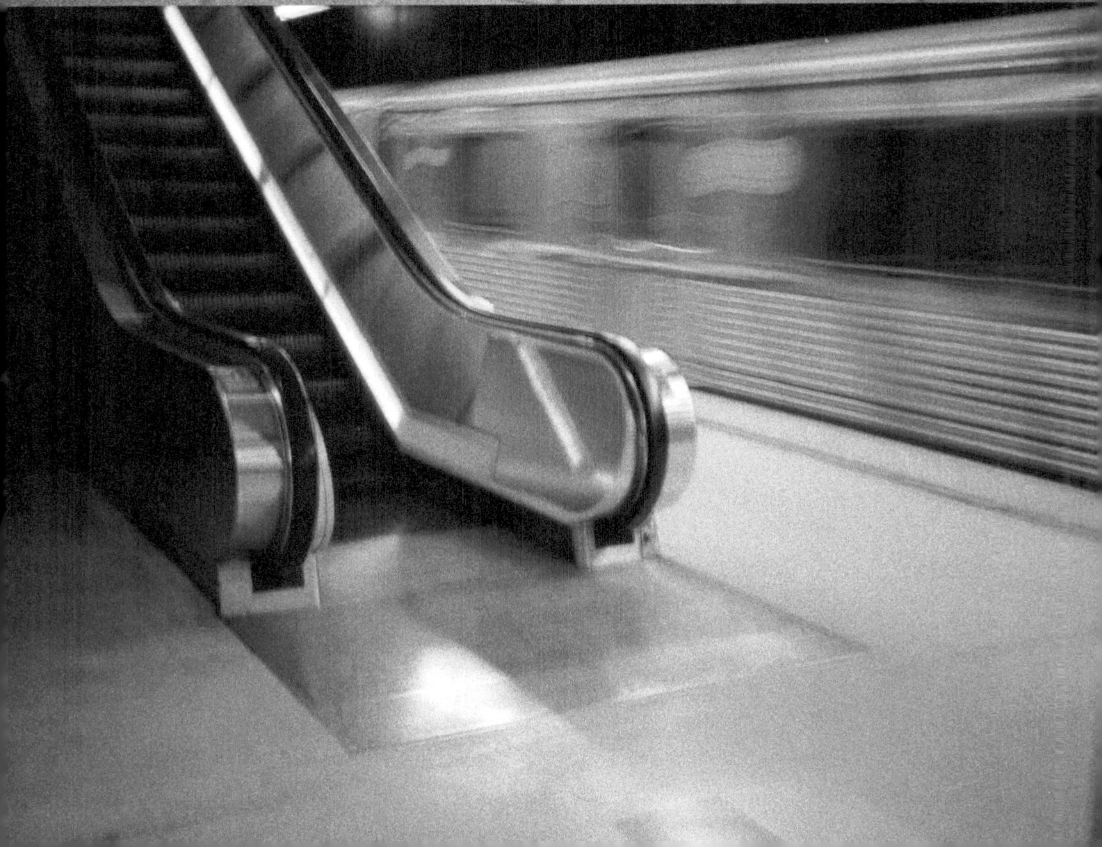

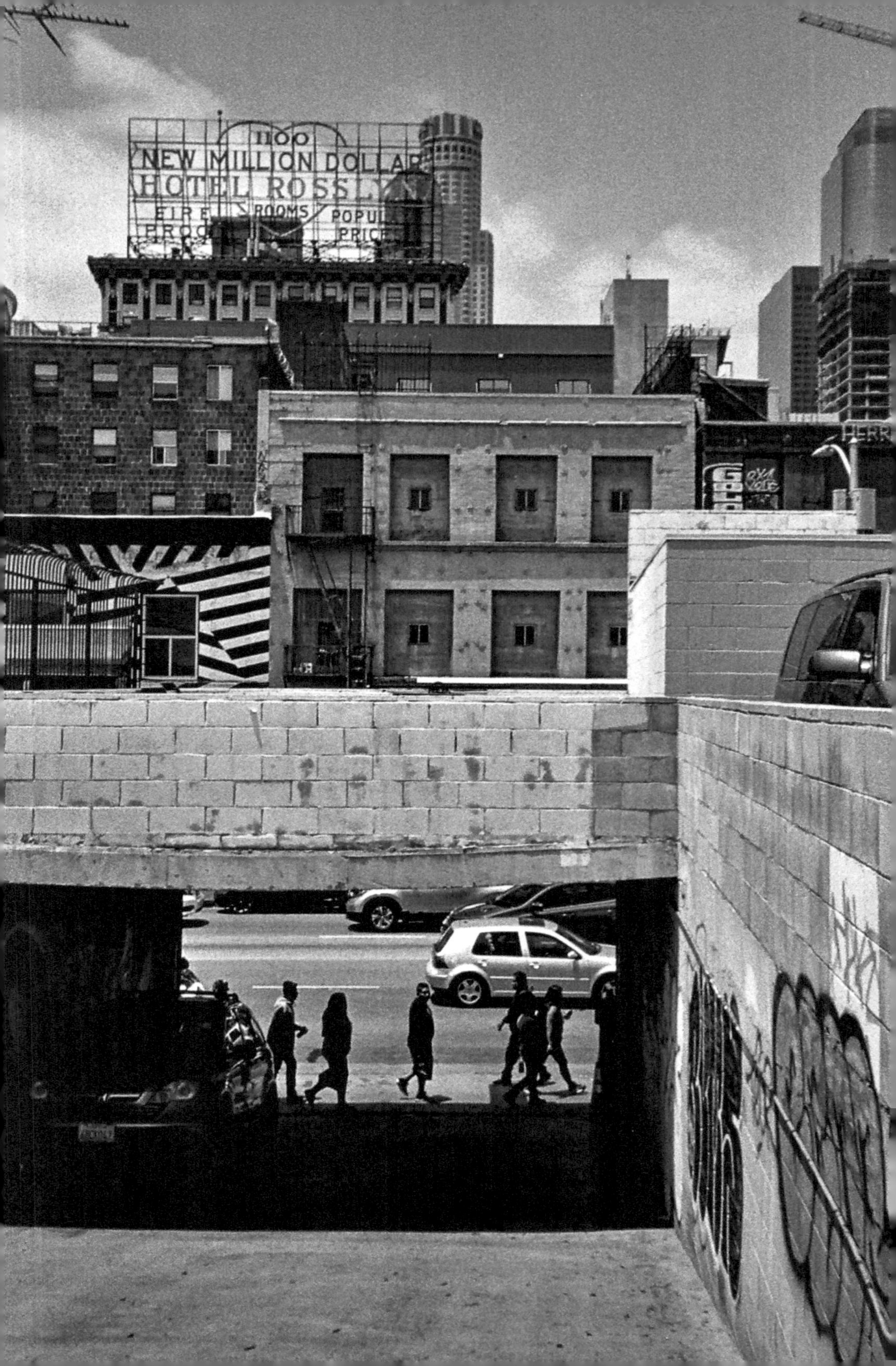
1100
NEW MILLION DOLLAR
ROOMS

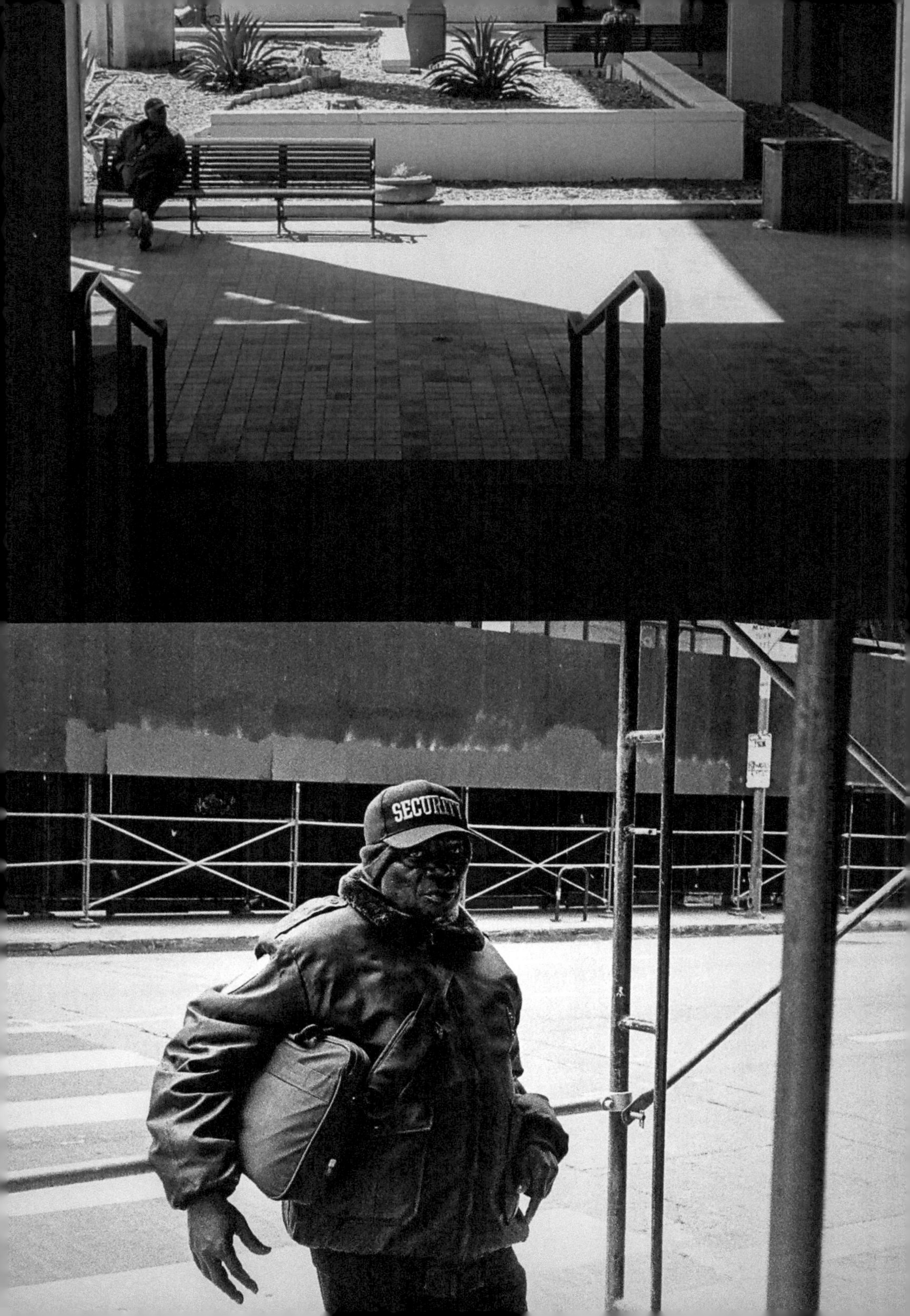
SECURITY

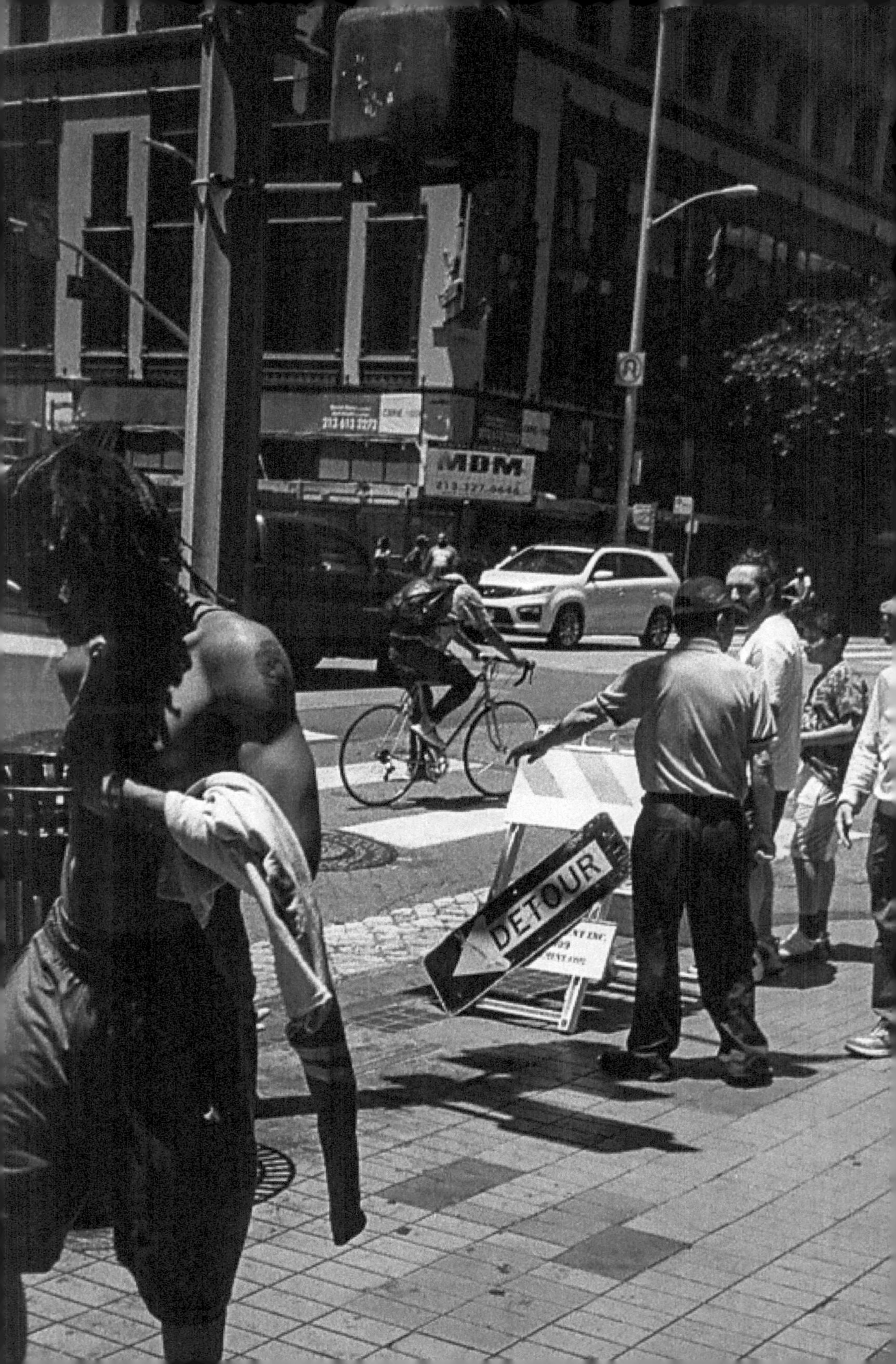
MDM
DETOUR

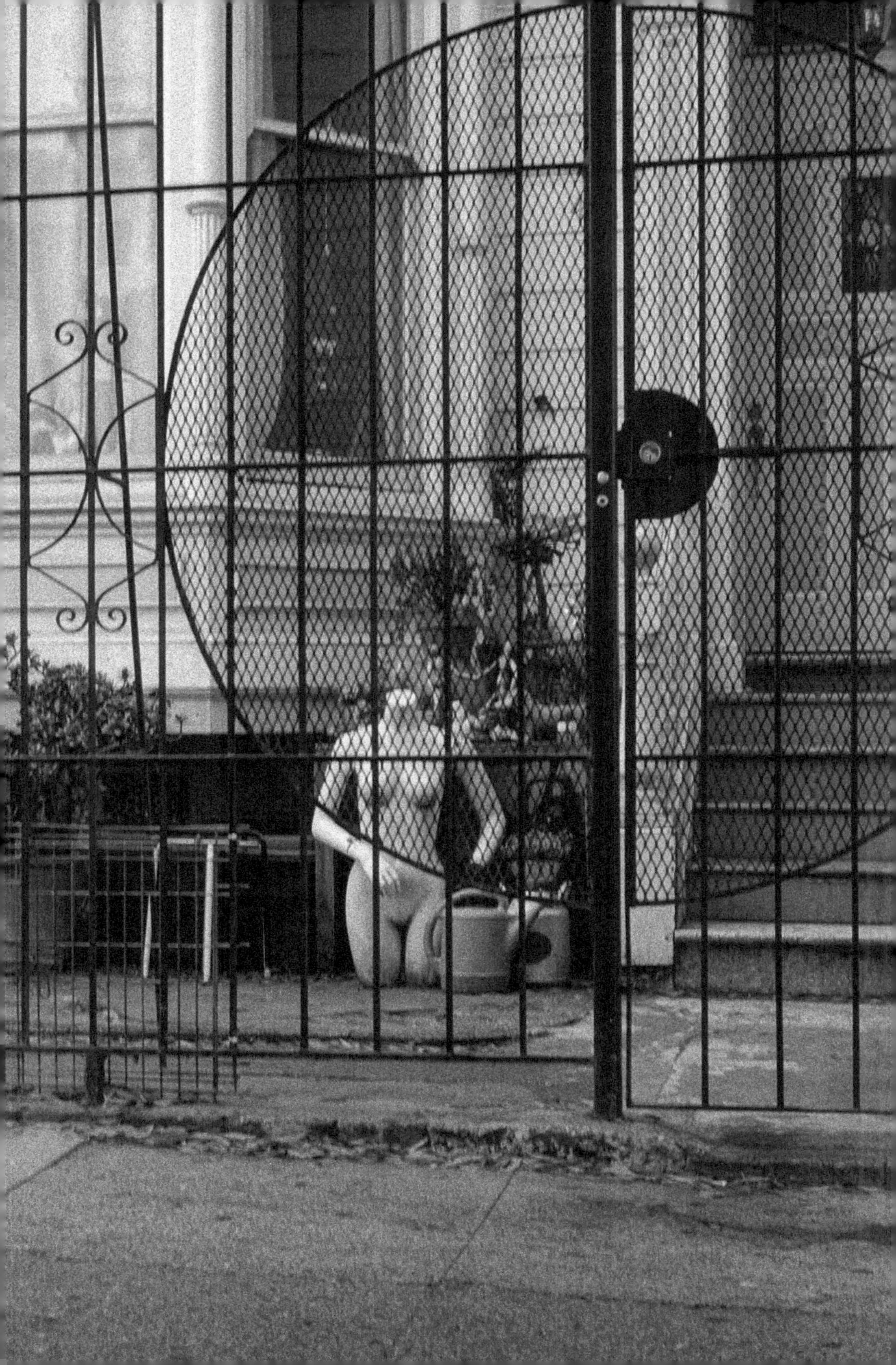

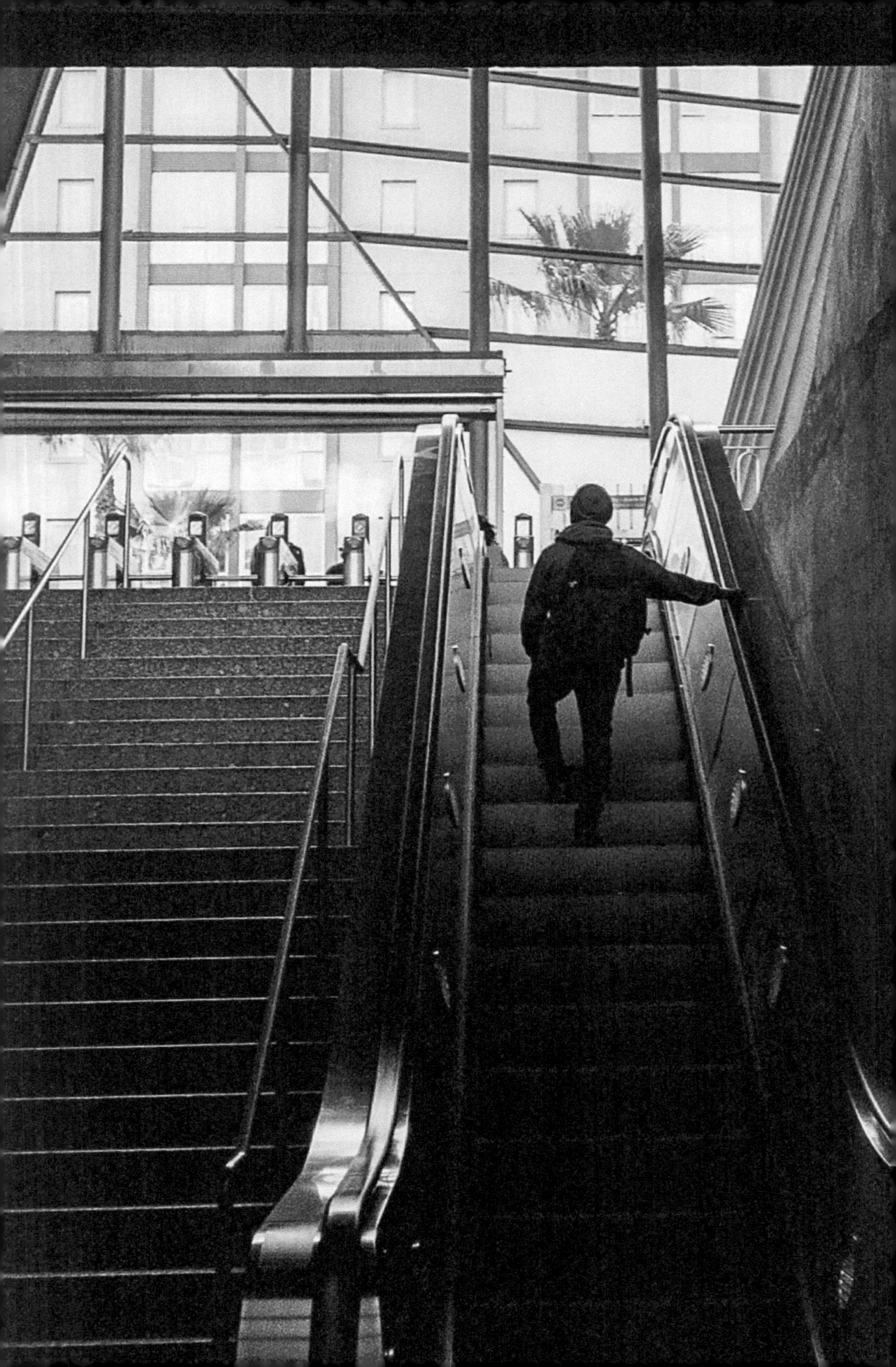

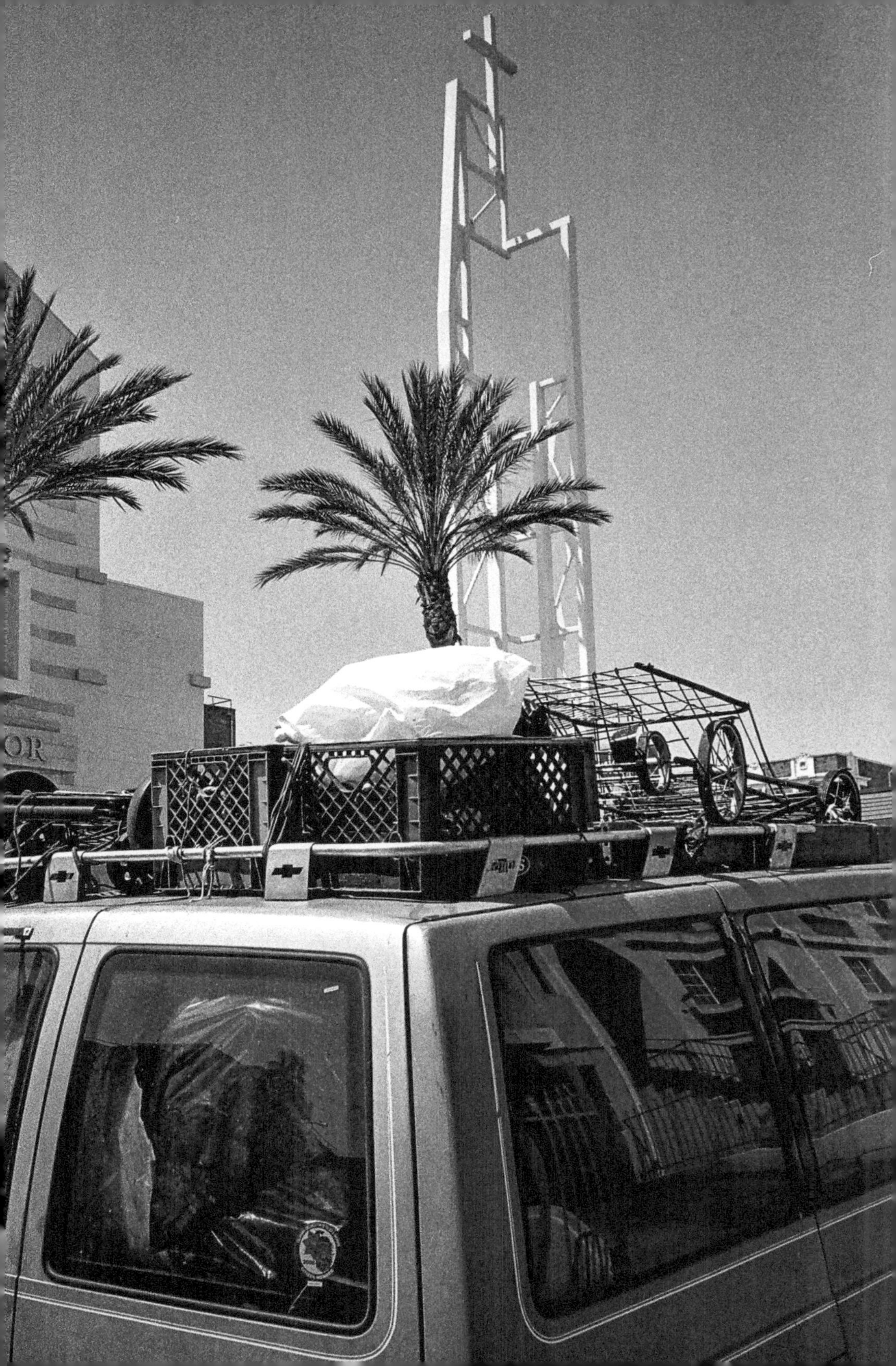

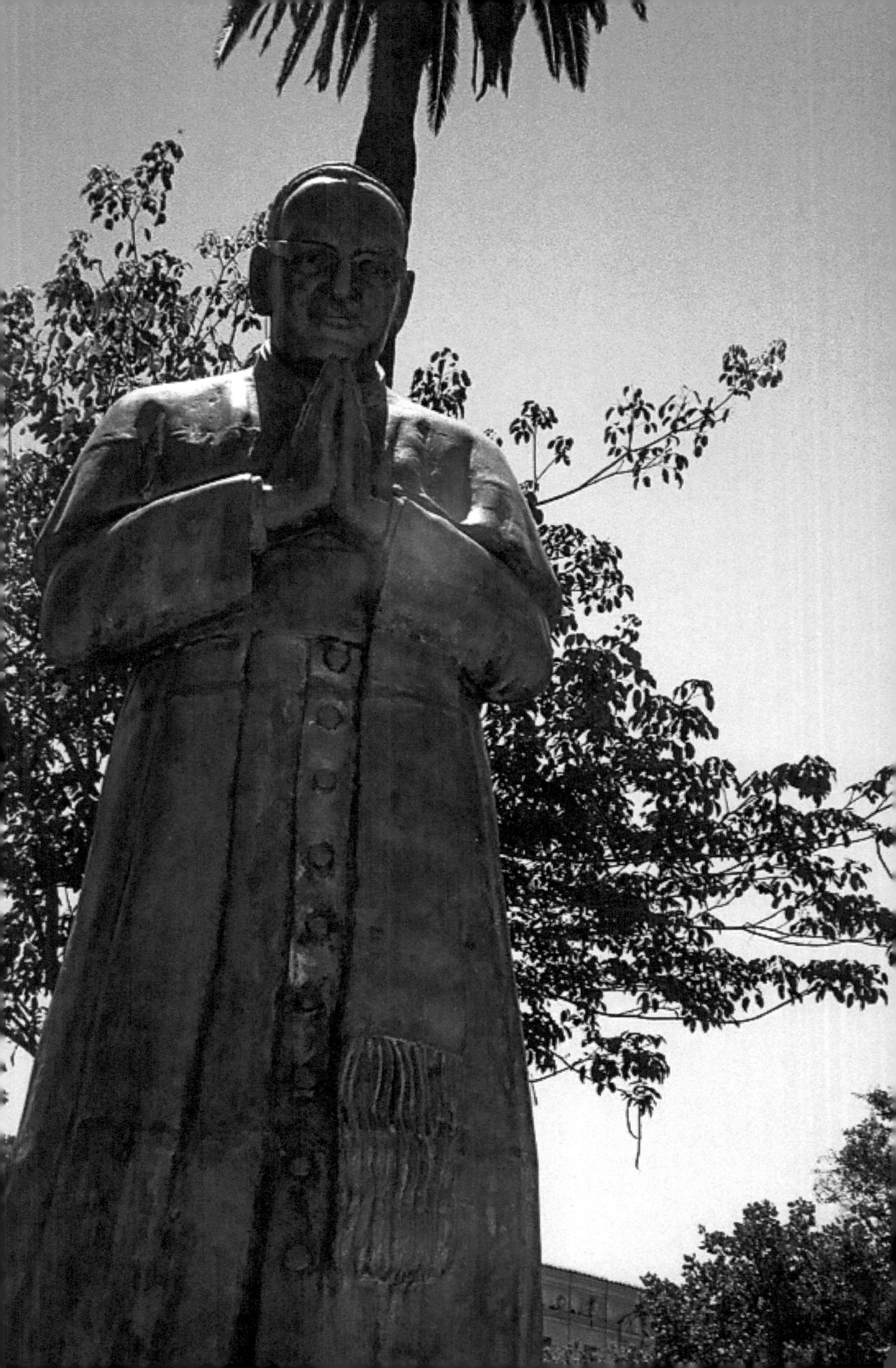

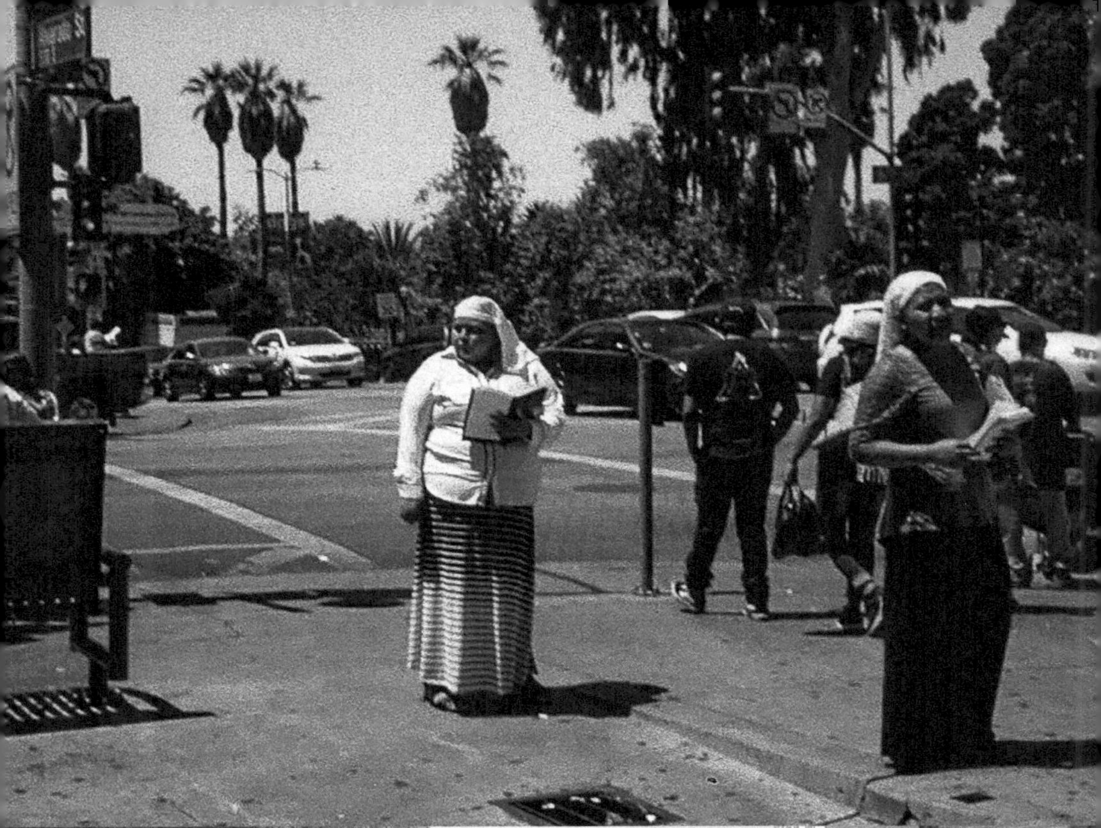

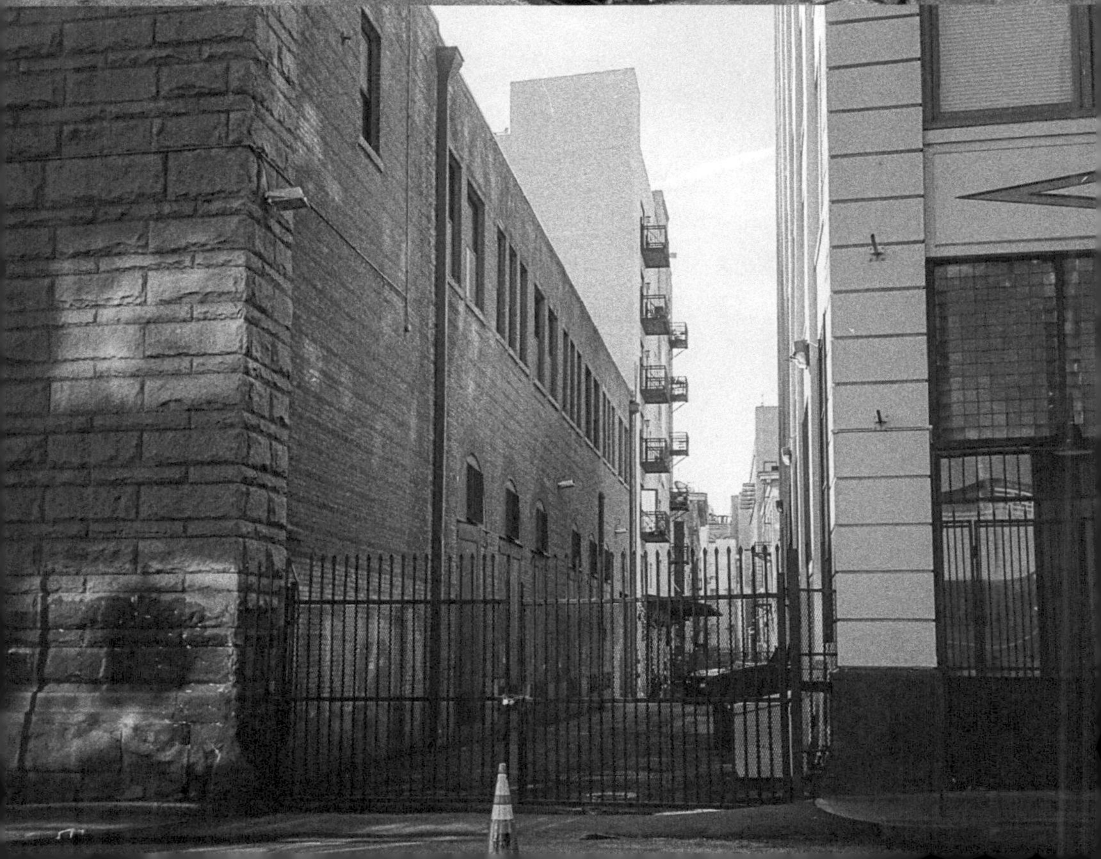

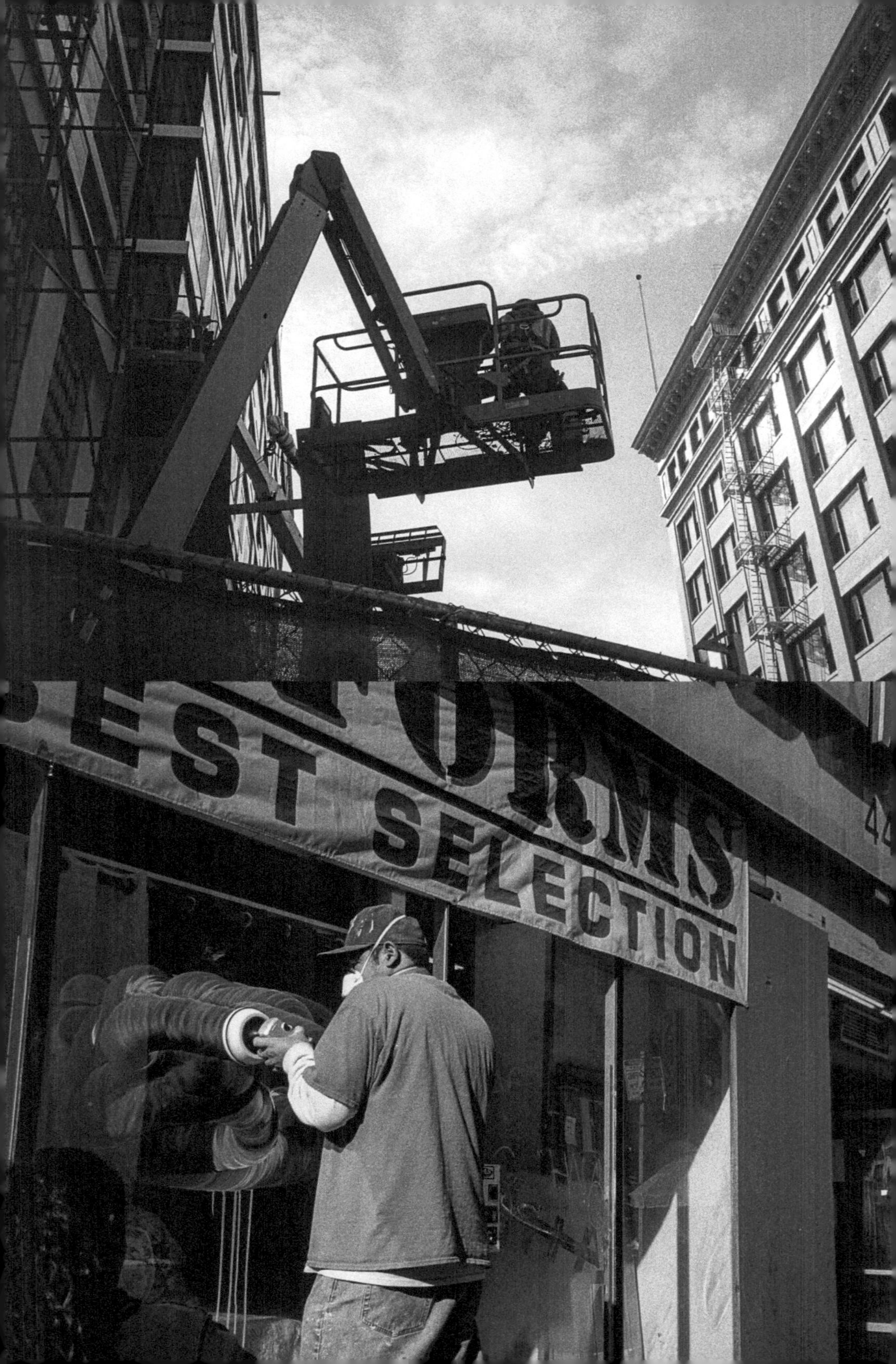
EST
SELECTION

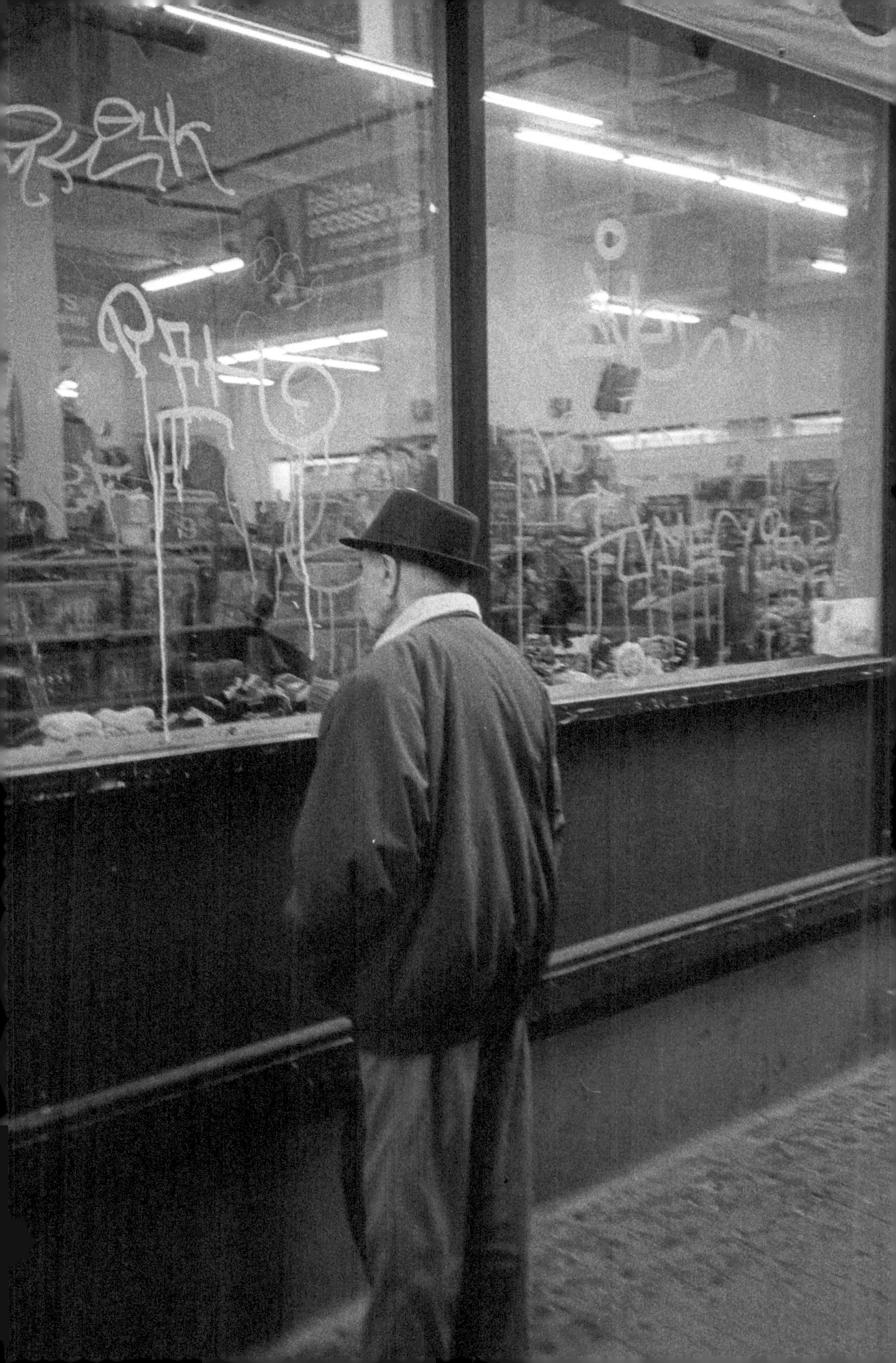

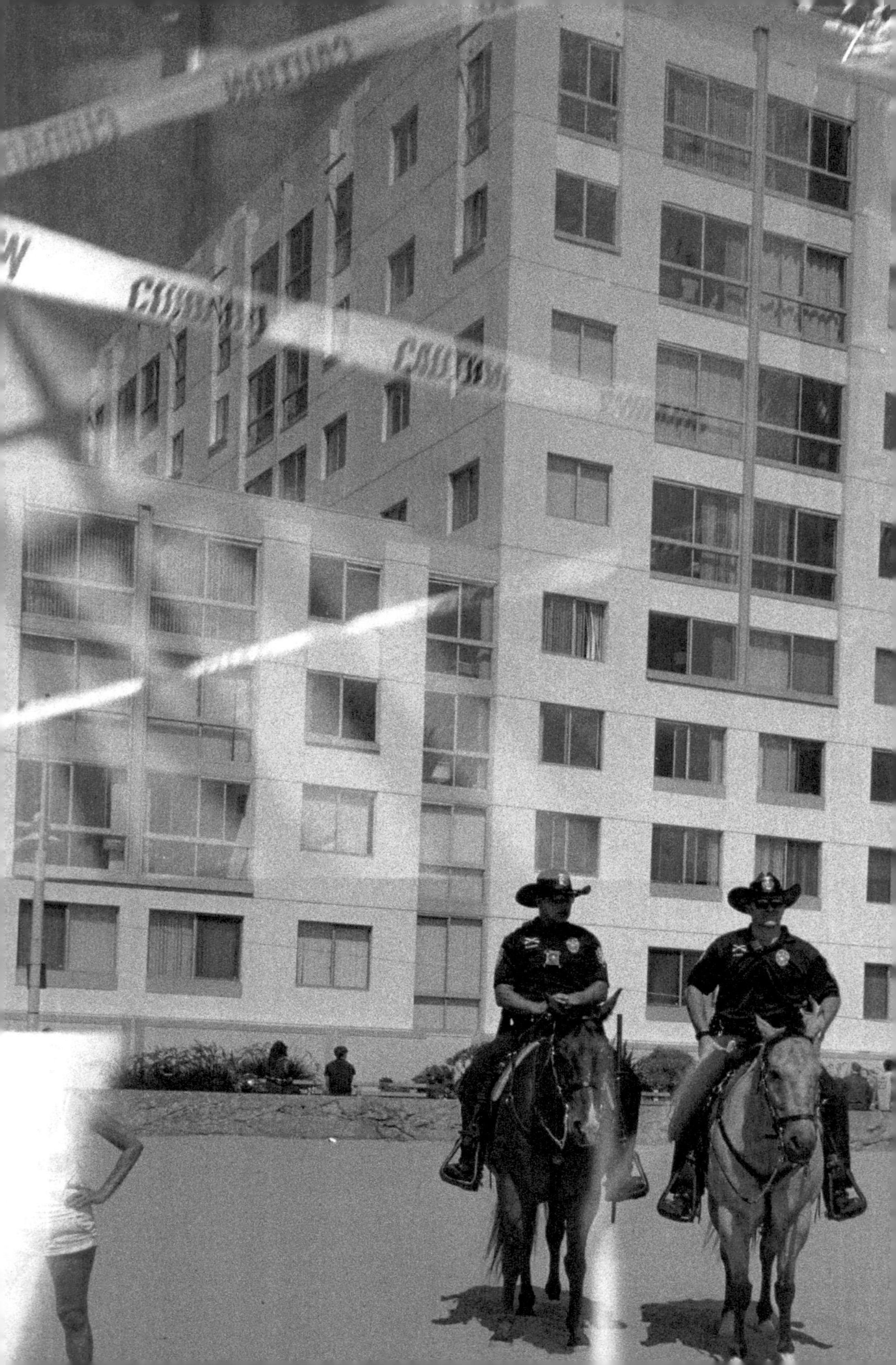

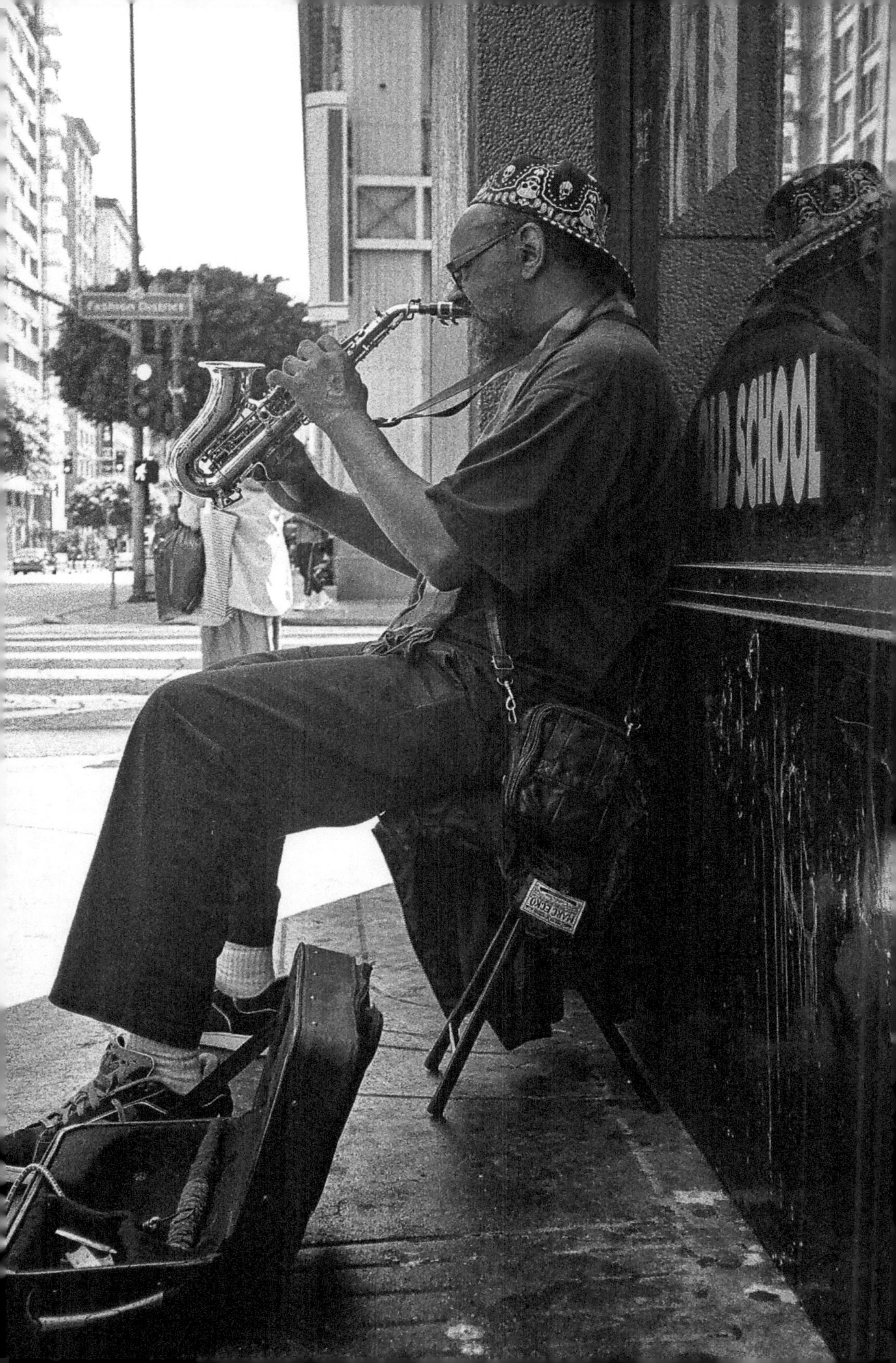
SCHOOL

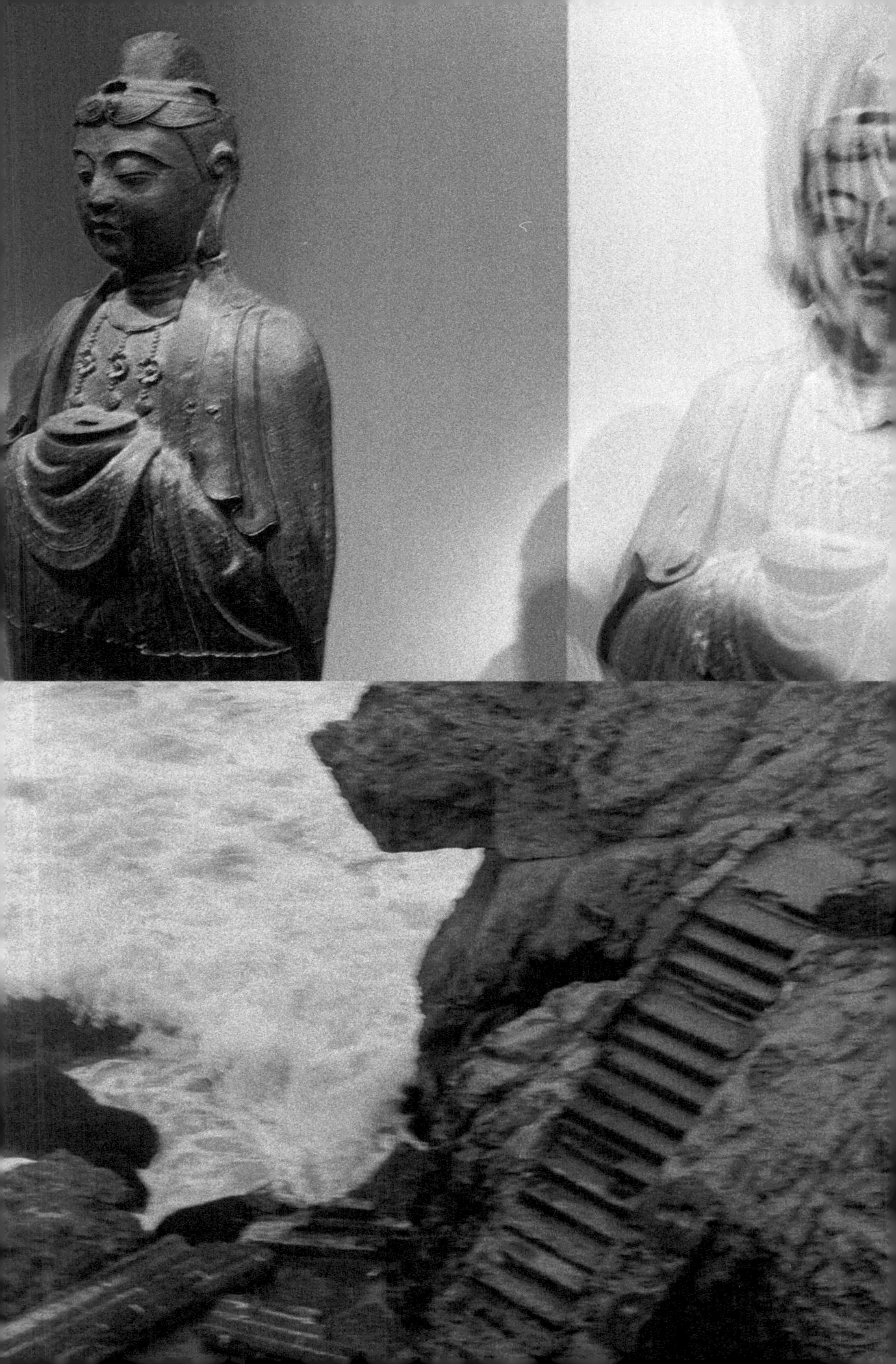

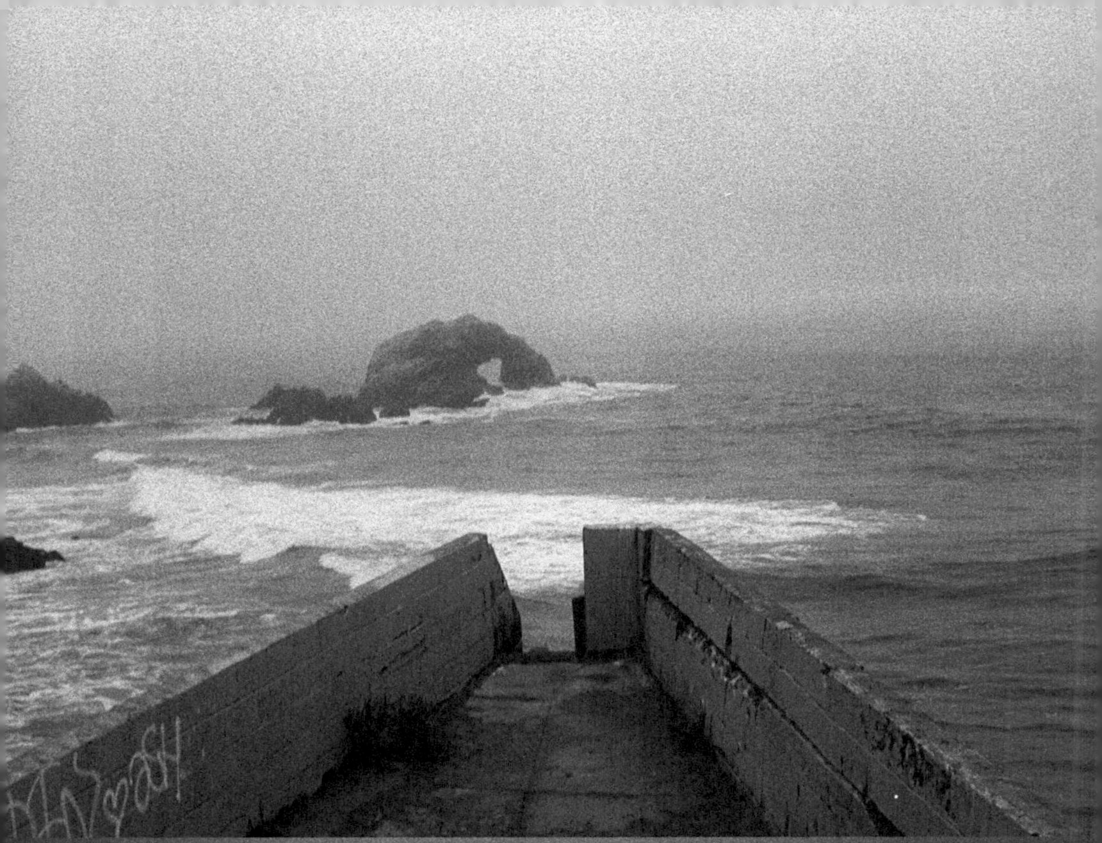

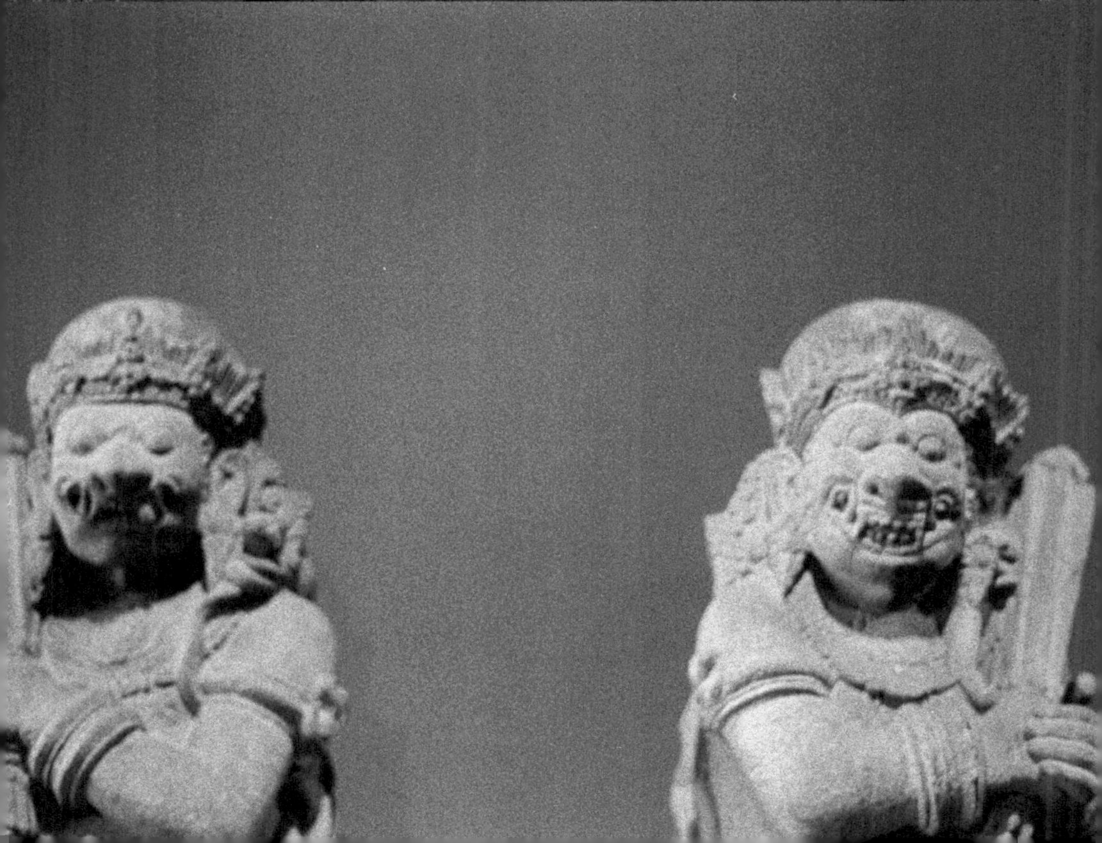

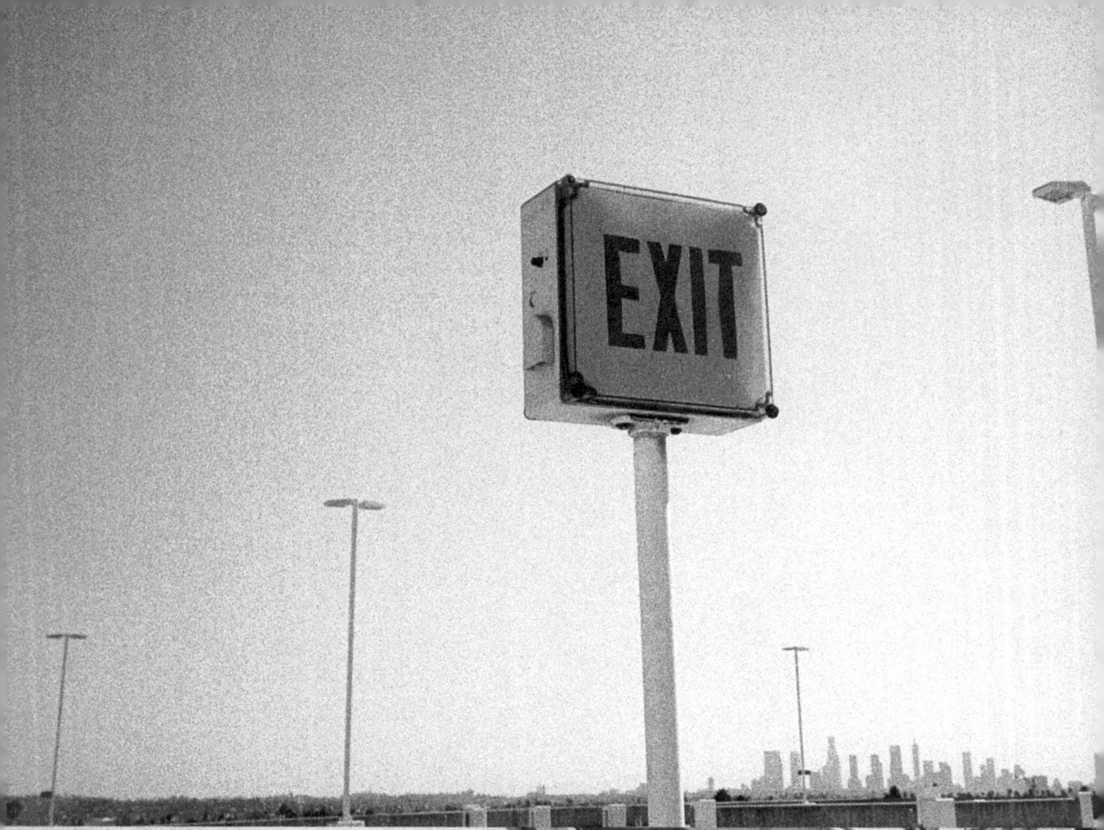
EXIT
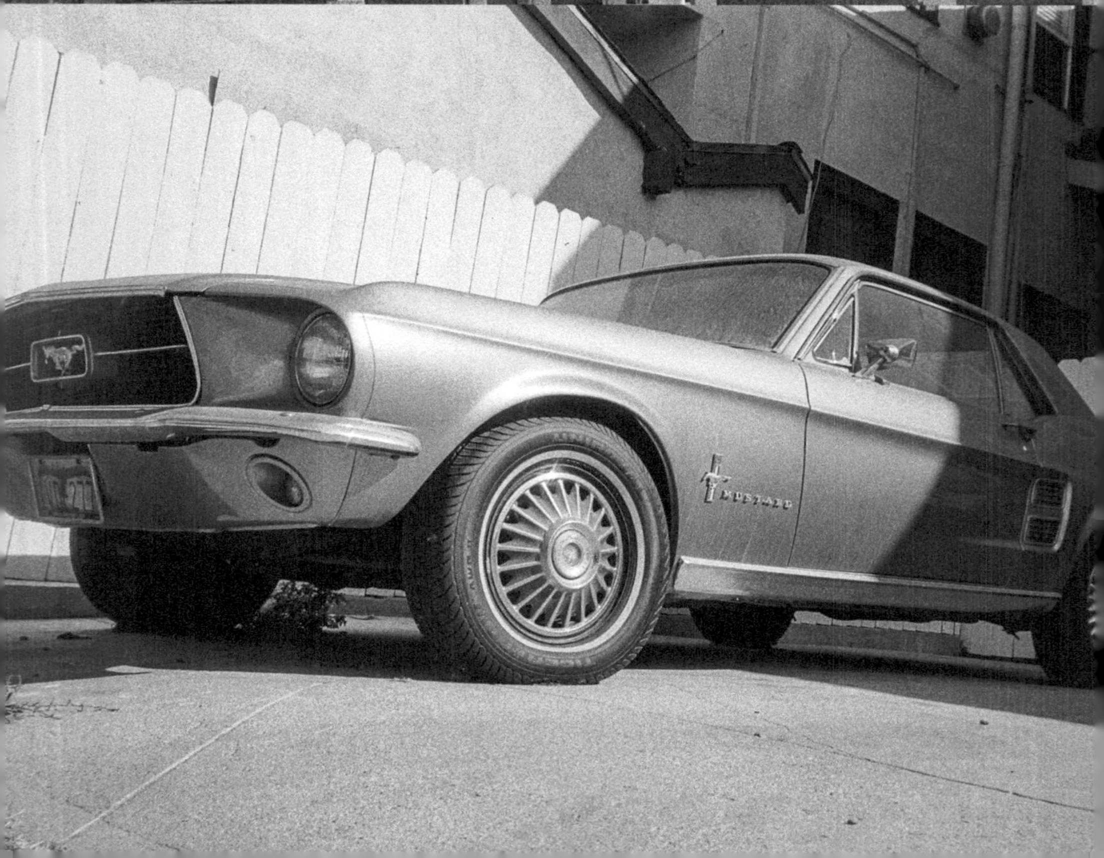

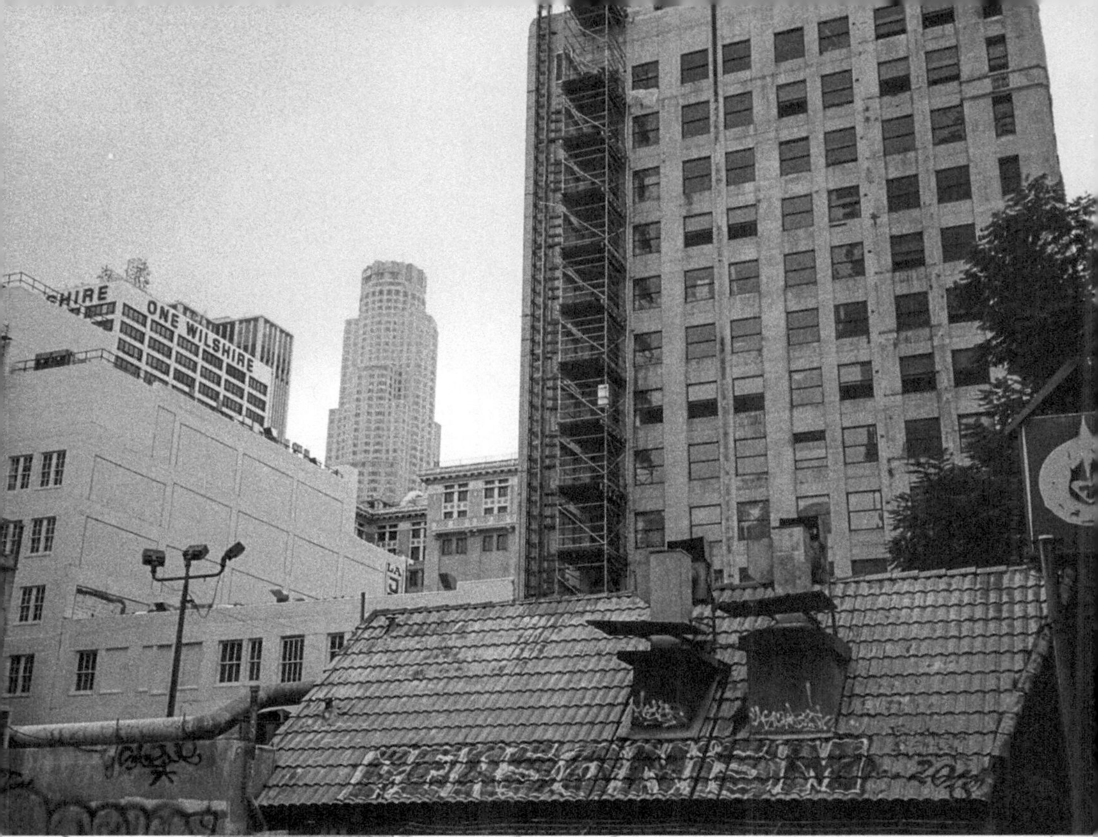
SHIRE
ONE WILSHIRE

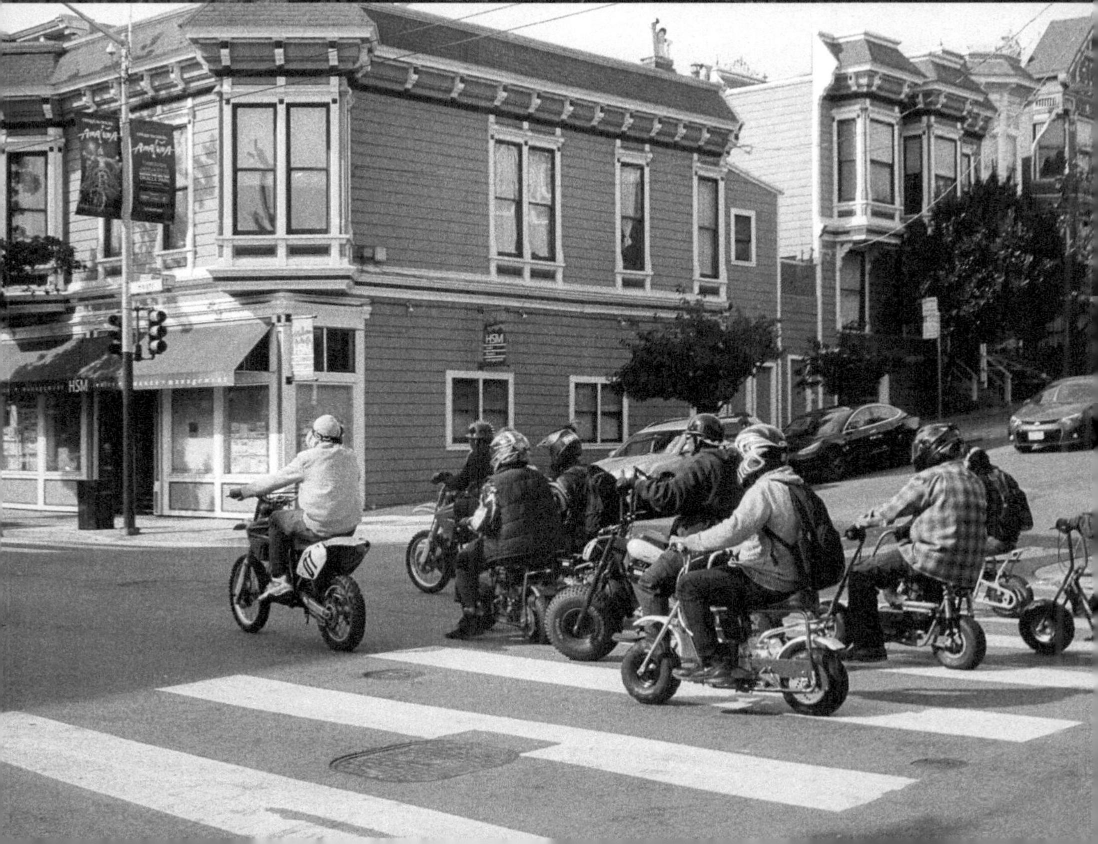
HSM
HSM

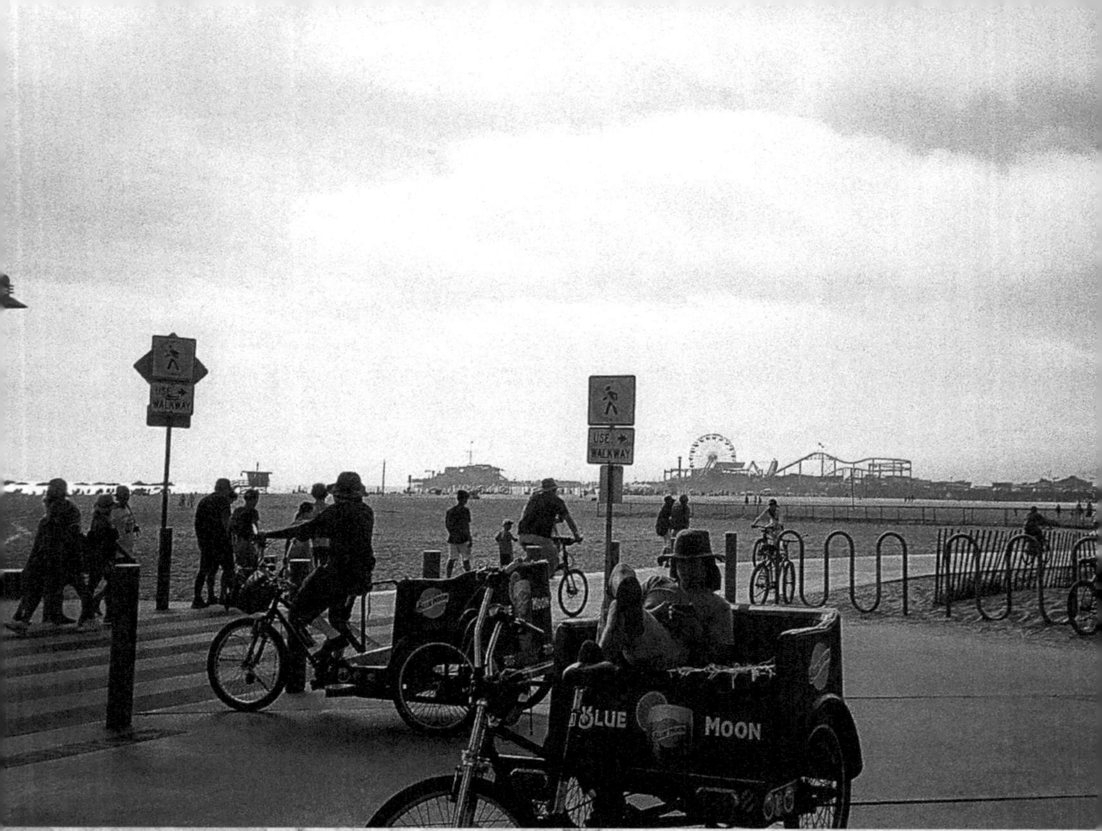
USE WALKWAY
USE WALKWAY
BLUE MOON

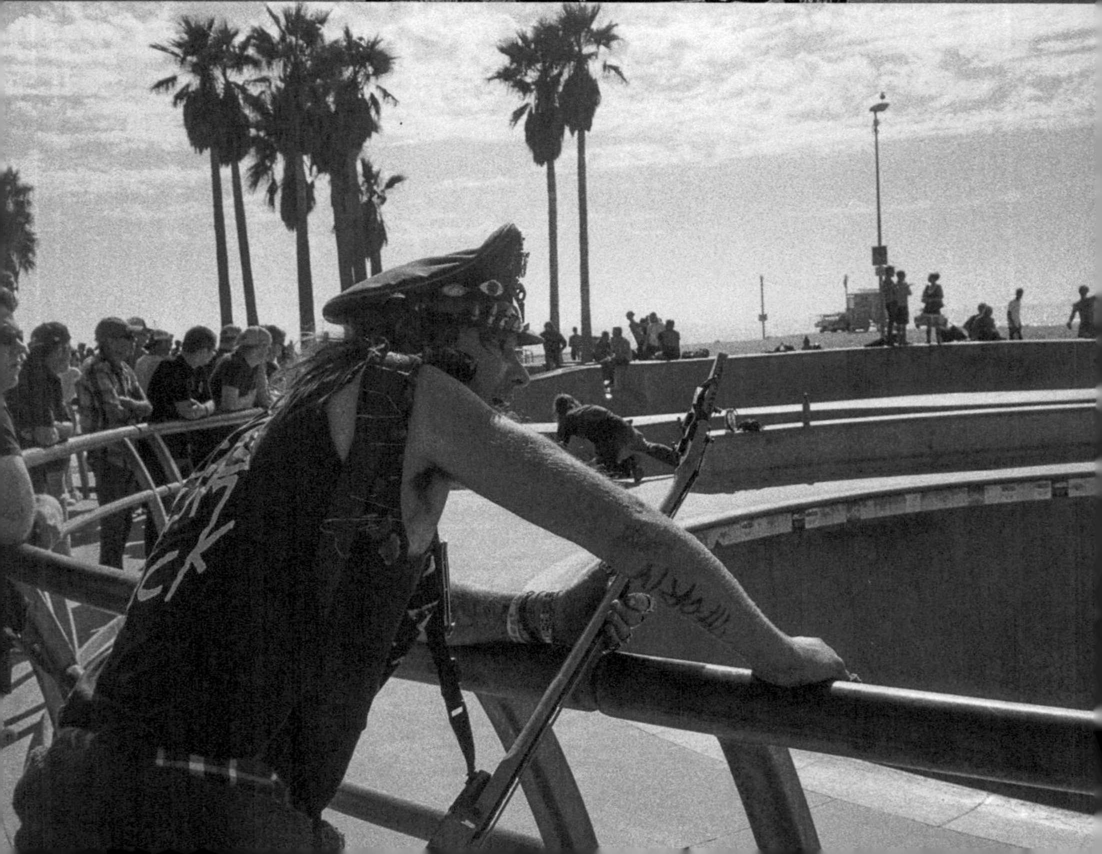

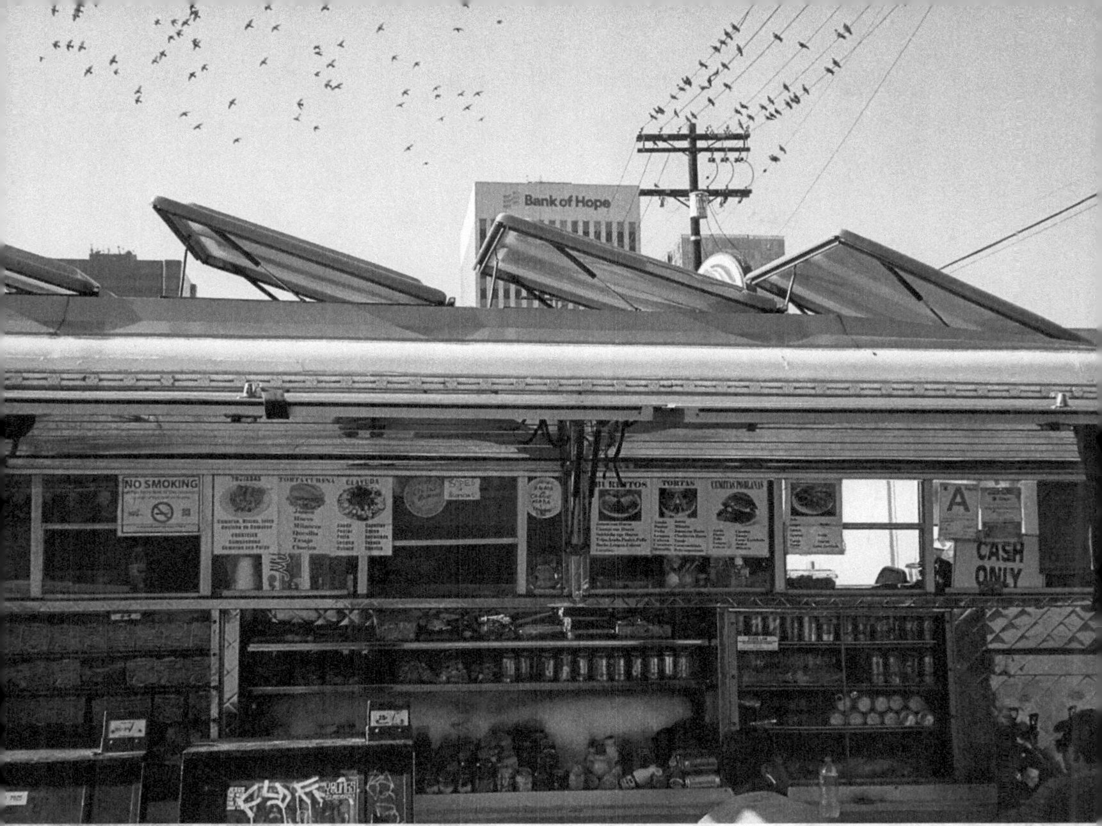
Bank of Hope
NO SMOKING
TORTAS
CASH ONLY

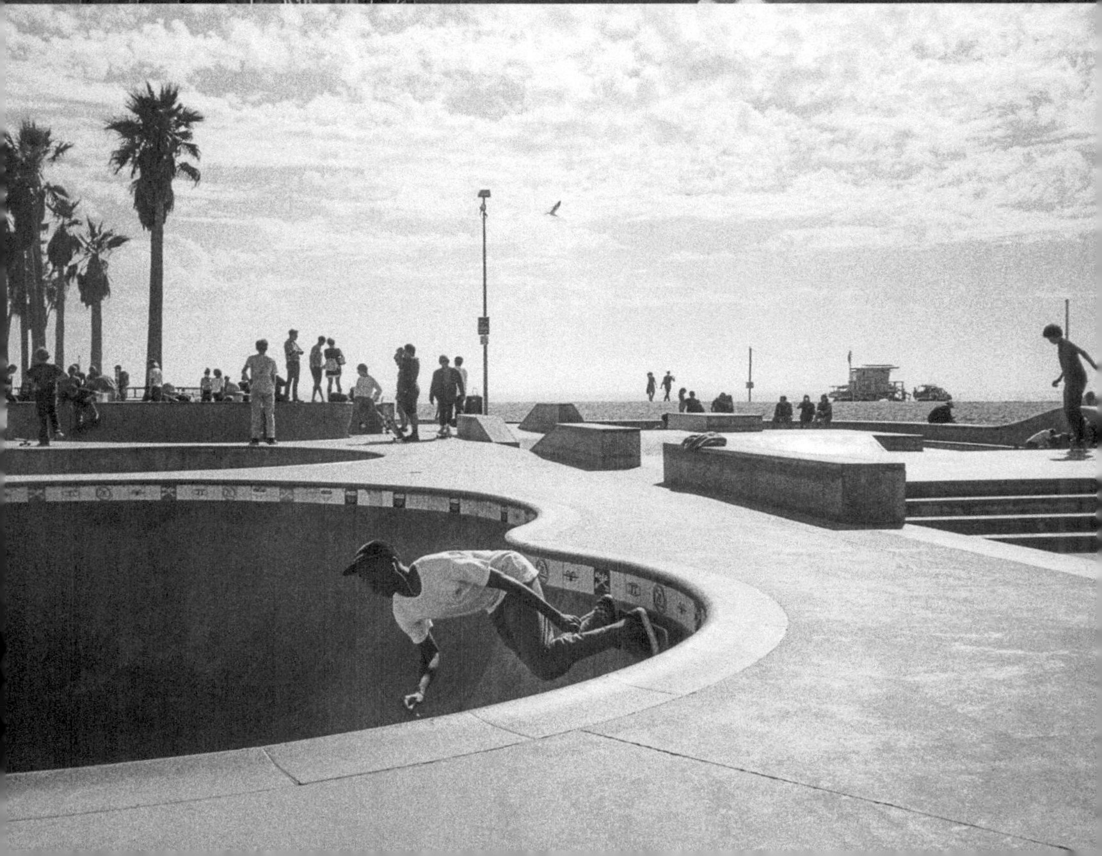

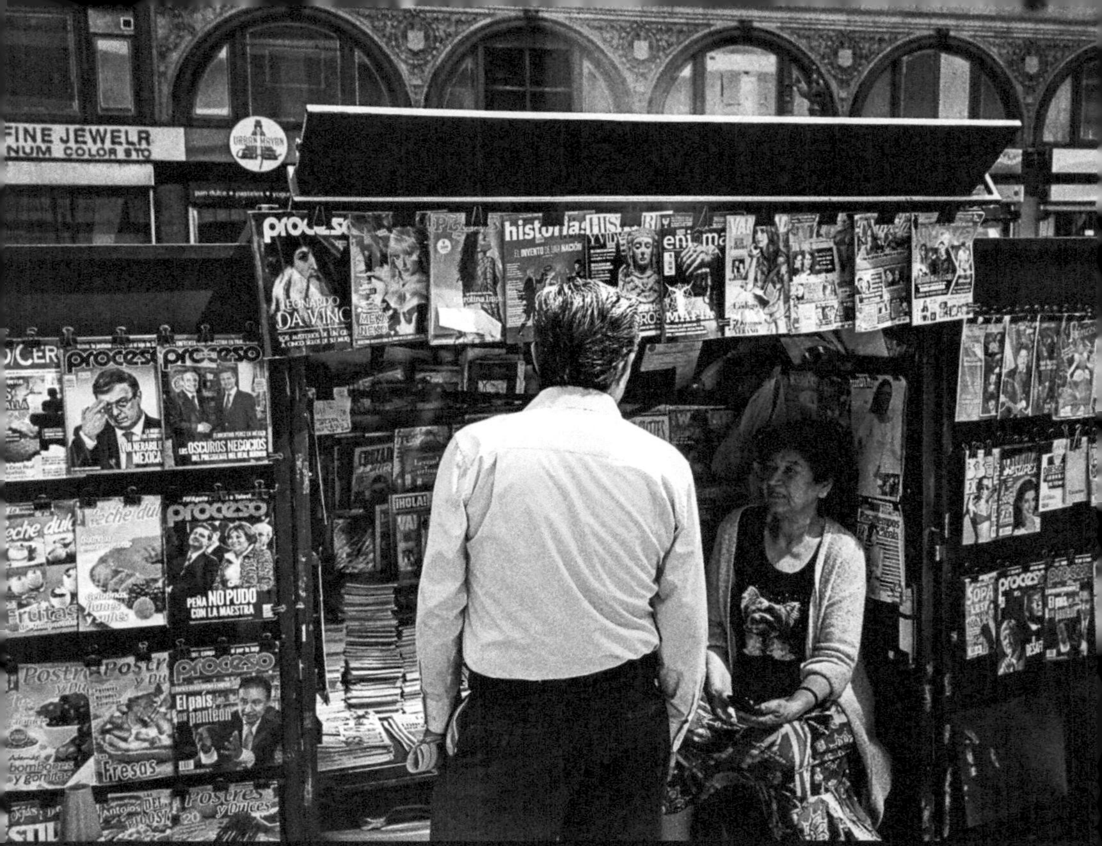
FINE JEWELR
NUM COLOR STO
proceso
historias
EL INVENTO DE UNA NACIÓN
LOS OSCUROS NEGOCIOS
PEÑA NO PUDO CON LA MAESTRA
El país
panteón
¡HOLA!
Fresas
Postres y Dulces

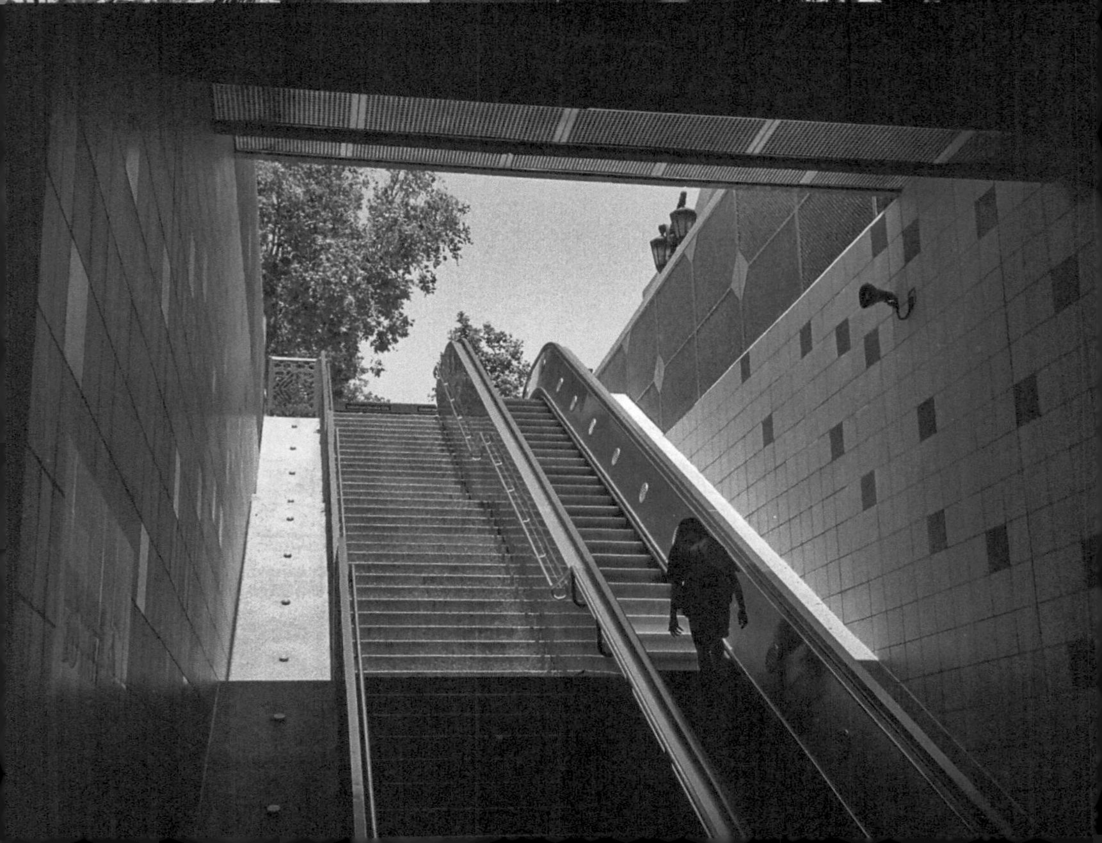

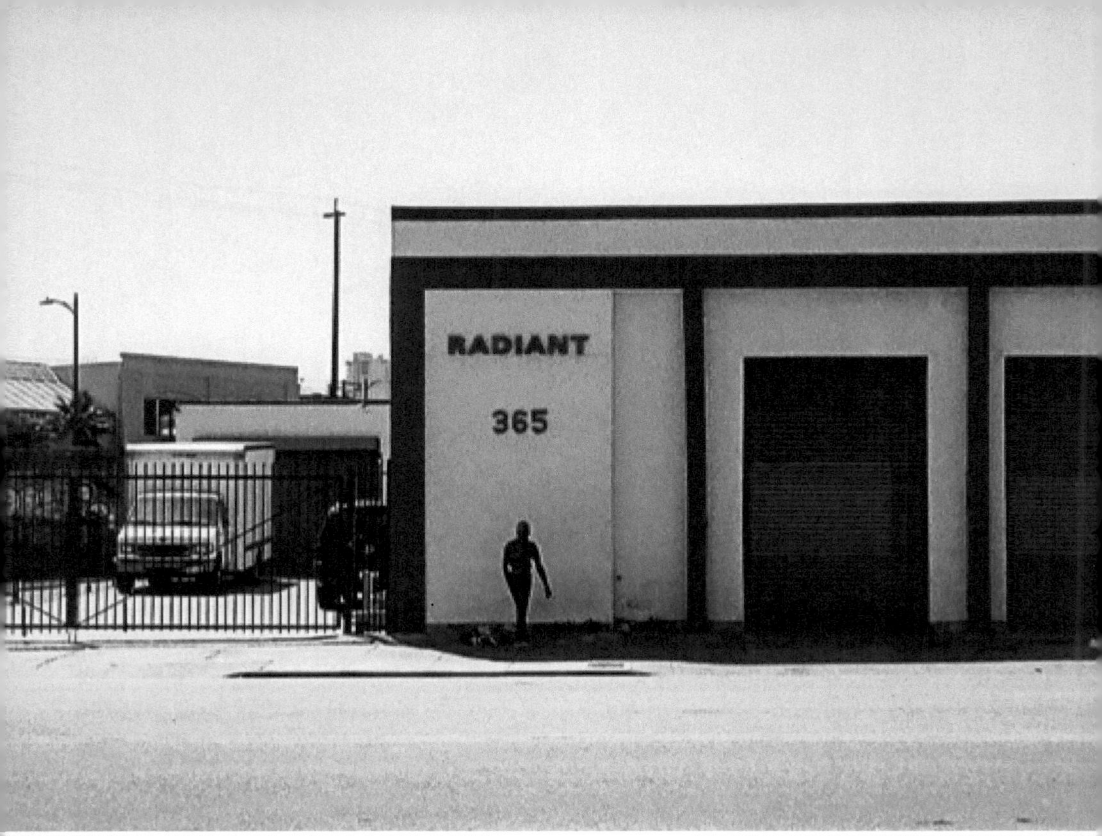
RADIANT
365

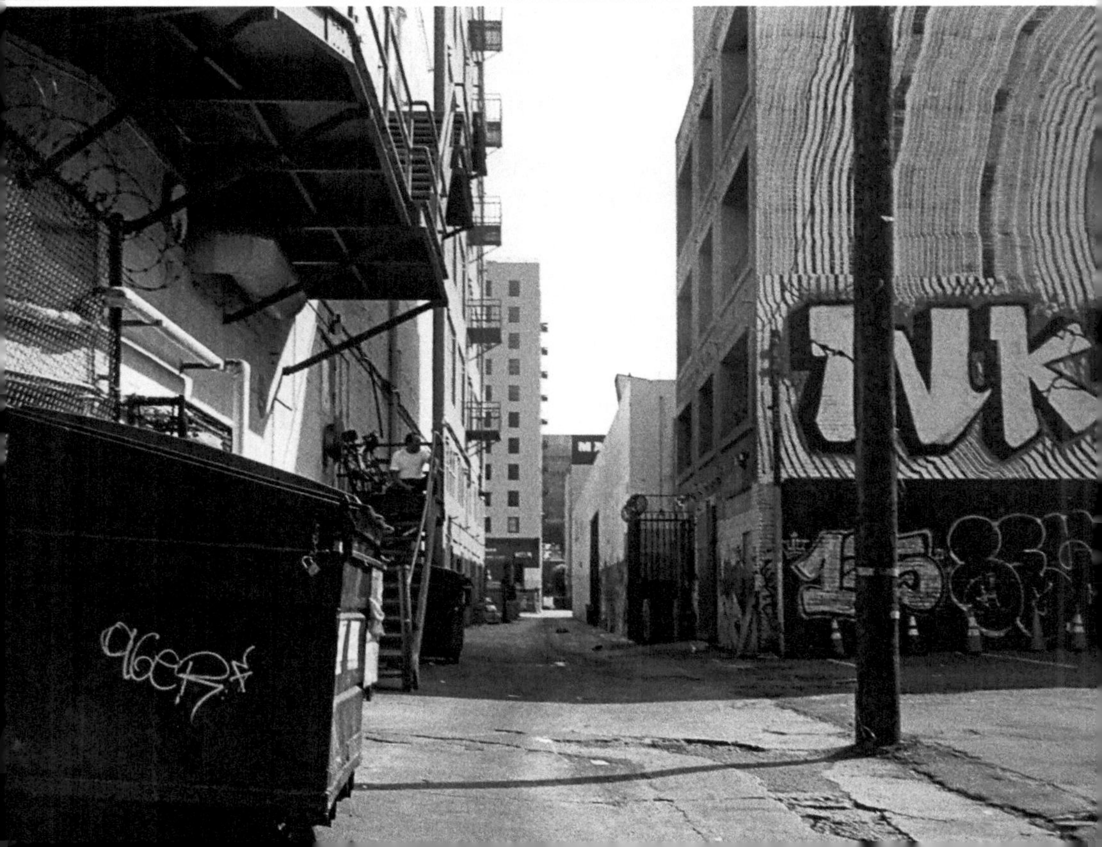

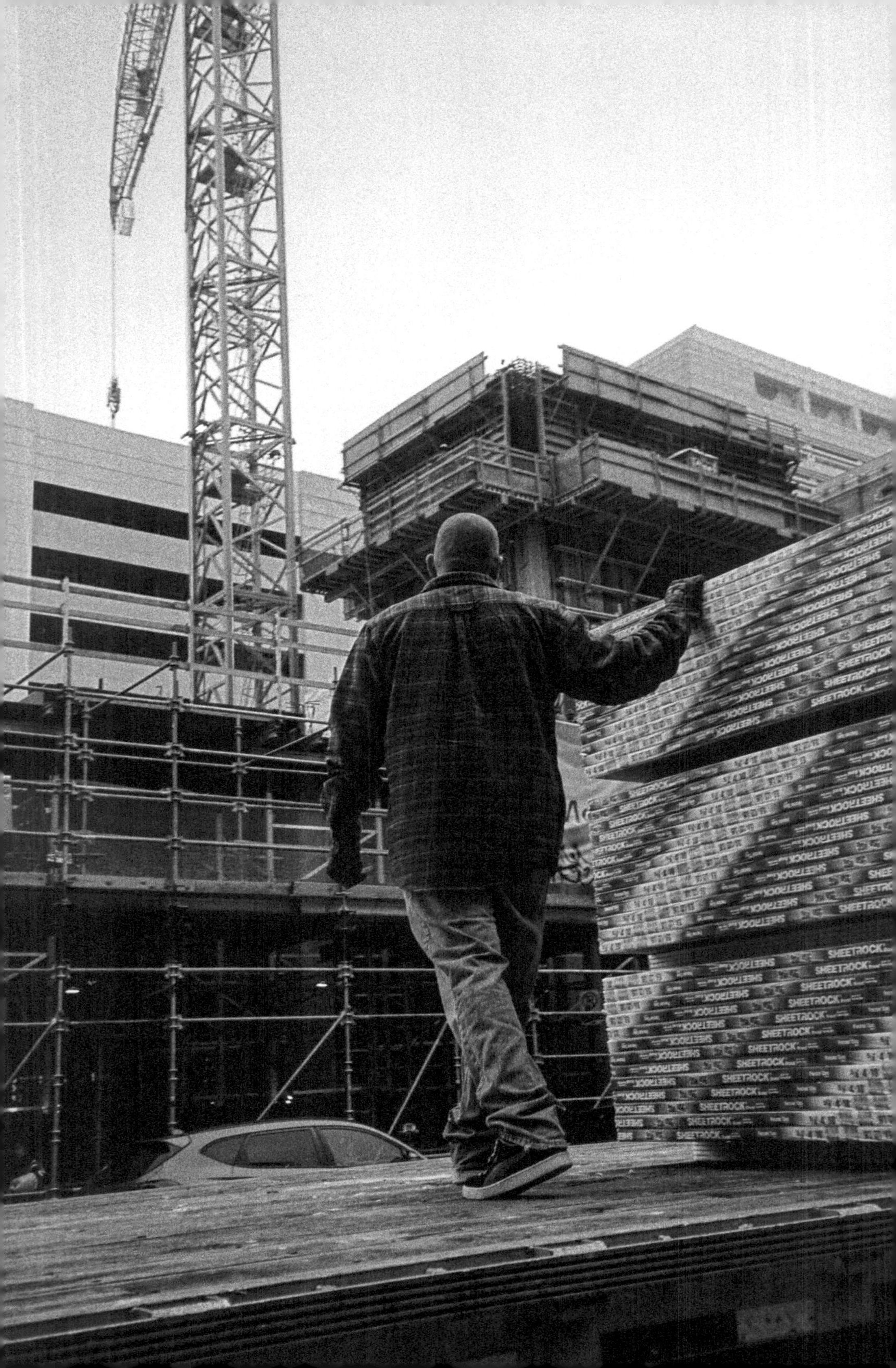
SHEETROCK

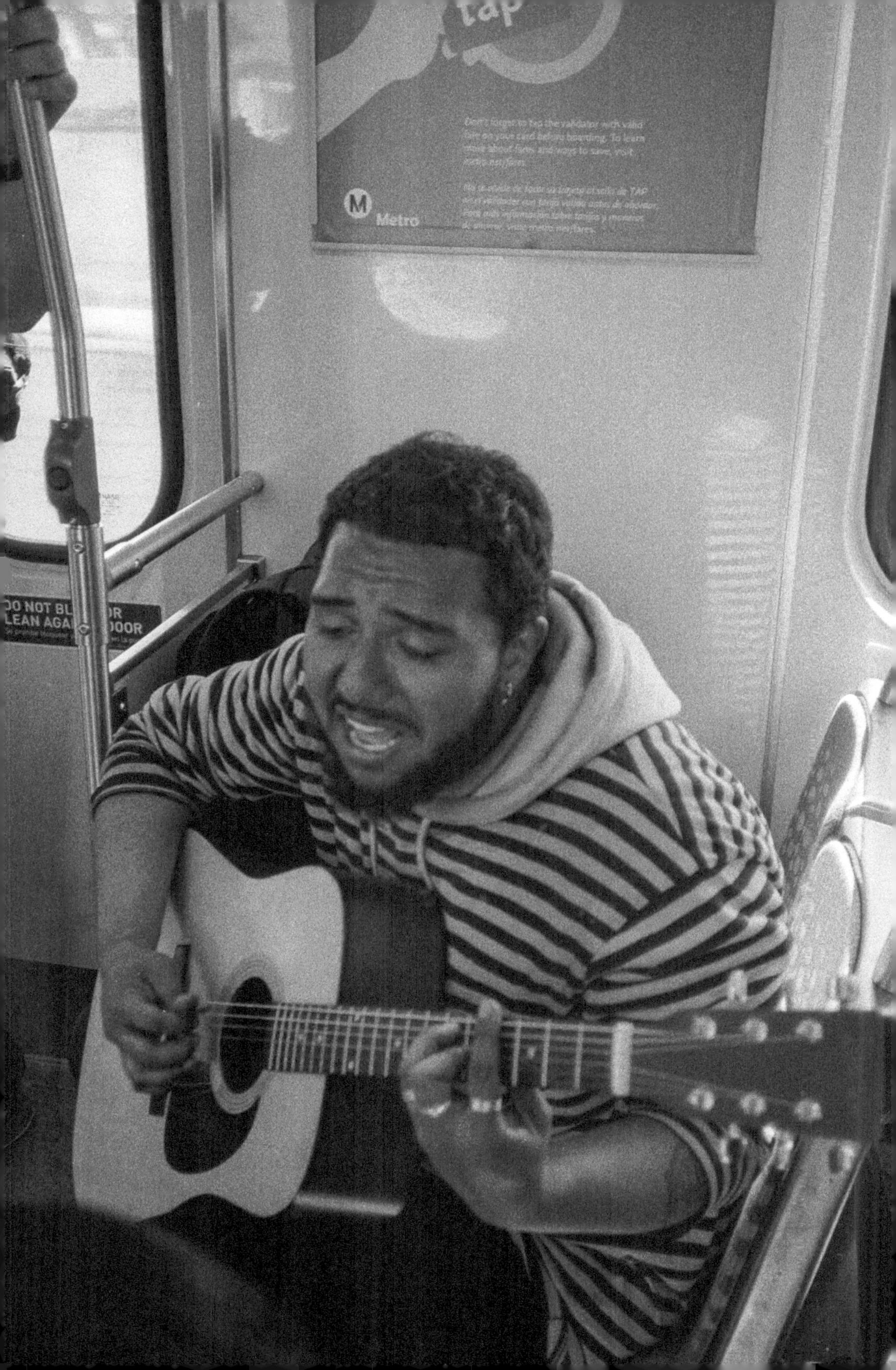
tap
Metro

www.ingramcontent.com/pod-product-compliance
Lightning Source LLC
Chambersburg PA
CBHW040342220526
45473CB00009B/2769
* 9 7 9 8 6 1 0 3 8 3 9 4 1 *